I0161515

Iliya Boris Englin

Indo-European Societies and Zoroastrianism –

Unravelling Convergent Trends in Historical Distortion

ISBN 0-9582711-2-7

EnglinSolutions Ltd NZ ® 2007.

Distributed in association with www.amazon.com

Cover Art: "The Promise of Zarathushtra" – I B Englin ®
2001

In Honoured Memory of My Mentor, Sergei Halafoff

Foreword

This offering synthesizes a number of concepts, poorly addressed in conventional teaching of history.

I am not a professional historian and say so on purpose. Professionals suffer from many occupational illnesses that impair their ability to analyze the subject of this book.

Some academics fear controversy that may interfere with their employment. Others are held captive by cultural prejudices. Most suffer from that gravest of scholarly diseases, an irrational conservatism that binds them to beliefs long discredited by facts.

My study of history began when I was growing up in Moscow, the capital of then USSR. The treatment of history under that regime deserves a treatise of its own – but suffice it to say that in the year when the Soviet power collapsed, the history examination for university entrance had to be cancelled, nation-wide. In that year two versions of history became available to students – one from official textbooks and another from "elsewhere". Needless to say, the two versions agreed on very little.

In USSR students of history had no access to independent sources. They had to interpret what they learned by subtracting the predictable leanings of official propaganda by "reading between the lines".

Whilst that was mostly a simple task, occasionally official textbooks not only offered a skewed analysis but falsified facts altogether. A sceptical Russian learned to look for discontinuities and inconsistencies. Some subjects, such as the French Revolution, had to be discarded as impossible to image from behind a curtain of lies. Soviet historians accepted that their understanding of history was punctuated by areas of discontinuity.

All that was known and understood. But when I resumed my studies in the free world, I was dismayed to learn that its historians also espouse distortions. A diligent student is able to source alternative views, but the uncritical "masses" are taught history heavily skewed by racism, Marxism or some other "ism".

History was not the only victim of the Soviet regime – its heretics in "hard" sciences also lived short and brutish lives. Soviet ideologues once banned studies in genetics and information technology – portentously so, as failure to develop both of these fields played a major role in the ultimate collapse of the Soviet colossus. Like the Nazi pseudo-science, the vandalism of Marxist "theoreticians" is often cited as classic flaw of totalitarianism.

Now let's examine two examples of how the academia of the pluralist and democratic West rewards those who challenge established dogma.

The first is one of the most shameful episodes in anthropology – a discipline, if one may use this term, rich in embarrassing episodes.

For much of the twentieth century anthropology was under the spell of Margaret Mead, who once spent some time on the Pacific island of Samoa. Her investigations, based on interviews with local teenage girls, led Mead to conclude that indigenous Samoan culture was blessed by a totally un-European attitude to sex – the natives performing it liberally, plentifully and joyfully. She became something of a cult figure for her analysis, which implied that the stilted European attitude to sex is abnormal and unhealthy. Two subsequent generations erected a tall edifice of pseudo-science, resting on Mead's depiction of sexual utopia.

I quote the heretic, who chose to challenge those findings some fifty years later:

In 1978 I wrote to Dr Mead offering to send her the draft of the refutation on which I was working. Unfortunately, she died on the 15th of November that year without ever having seen it. When it was finally published by Harvard University Press in 1983, the consternation, especially in America, was enormous. Without warning, the Meadian reverie about Samoa had been shattered. For American anthropologists, as one of them remarked, this was "a seismic event", and, as they surveyed the fallen masonry, the embarrassment of those whose beliefs had been so rudely shaken quickly turned to fury against the antipodean Antichrist who had so desecrated their sanctum sanctorum. In no time at all, as one observer has recorded, there were many who seemed willing to tear me "limb from limb". Things reached their apogee in November 1983, when, during the 82nd meeting of the American Anthropological Association, a special session devoted to the evaluation of my refutation was held. It was attended by more than a thousand. The session began conventionally enough, but when the general discussion started, it degenerated into a delirium of vilification. One eye-witness has described it as "a sort of grotesque feeding frenzy"; another wrote to me saying "I felt I was in a room with... people ready to lynch you". This then is the kind of fanatical behaviour that is released in the zealots of a closed system of thought when one of their principal certainties has been effectively challenged.

What's more, later that same day, a motion denouncing my refutation as "unscientific" was moved, put to the vote, and passed. Yet, as a moment's thought discloses, the notion that the scientific status of a proposition can be settled by a show of hands at a tribal get-together is unscientific in the extreme.

I now come to what was for me the most unexpected of denouements. When I arrived back in American Samoa in 1987 I was introduced by Galea'i Poumele, the Samoan Secretary of Samoan Affairs, to a dignified Samoan lady whom I had never previously met. During my previous visits to Manu'a she had been living in Hawaii where she had gone with her family in 1962. She was Fa'apua'a Fa'amu, who, in 1926, had been Margaret Mead's closest Samoan friend. In 1987, at 86 years of age, she was still in full command of her mental faculties. Fa'apua'a's sworn testimony to Galea'i Poumele was that when Mead had insistently questioned her and her friend Fofoa about Samoan sexual behaviour, they were embarrassed, and – as a prank – had told her the exact reverse of the truth.

Dr Derek Freeman (from an address given at The Sydney Institute on July 9, 1996.)

The second episode I wish to cite concerns a supposedly rigorous and scientific discipline of internal medicine. In 1985 Drs Barry Marshall and Robyn Warren, two heretics from a teaching hospital in Western Australia, had suggested that many stomach ulcers are caused by a certain bacterium, subsequently named Helicobacter pylori. At that time approximately 50% of all surgery performed in major hospitals was related to the treatment of ulcers and their complications.

Their idea was first made available to the best brains of the medical profession in 1982 and published definitively by 1986.

Initially ignored outright, the authors were then reviled and derided. Despite Helicobacter being declared a Class I carcinogen by World Health Organization in 1994, it was not until the end of that decade that a patient presenting with symptoms related to the presence of Helicobacter could expect to be offered appropriate treatment. In 2007 many older clinicians still refuse to acknowledge what today amounts to clear-cut evidence of cause and effect.

This is not the place to describe how the careers of Helicobacter heretics were affected by their beliefs, but suffice it to say that the Nobel Prize Warren and Marshall richly deserved awaited twenty years to be awarded.

These two incidents, along with others that would take longer to describe, completed the cycle of my education. I found myself back where I began – with a Russian's innate distrust of all institutional propaganda.

My motivation for writing this book is to provoke a review of a vital undercurrent in Western history, without the distortions imposed by traditional teaching.

I offer this book to the reader without fear of unemployment or ridicule – I reap daily bread far from ivory towers.

Assuming the reader to be open-minded and clear-thinking, I had deliberately avoided conventional blights of historical texts such as incomprehensibly long footnotes and other impediments to transmission of ideas. Where digression is necessary, I kept it brief but retained in the body of the text.

It is not my purpose to establish that Zoroastrianism was – or is – the optimal ethical framework for any given society. I do nothing more than examine its influence on increasingly sophisticated societies of the past three millennia – an influence that remains hidden from common view to this day.

It is not surprising that we fail to learn from history. Unlike biologists, historians do not present a coherent, flowing story of social evolution. It is true that some of our past is lost irretrievably and cannot be reconstructed in a scientific manner. But many discontinuities in that landscape result from the blade of a censor's knife, rather than ravages of time.

That loudly says the following. Science, including the study of history, cannot progress without an ethical compass. Indeed, that is history's only defence against those who set out to mutilate it. A paramount precept of any ethical system is that truth is the only way forward, in science above all.

In a wider biological context, ethical behaviour is about sustainability, mandating respect for an equilibrium that provides one's survival. Species that trample on their habitats vanish with remarkable speed, despite seeming success at the time of their ascendancy. We cannot do that equilibrium justice if we don't know how it came about – and history will tell us if we allow.

Through neglect of that knowledge even the

present civilisation could join a long list of vanished cultures that entertained themselves with delusions of omnipotence and immortality.

Introduction

Let's begin by identifying some important defects in the traditional teaching of history, areas that leave thoughtful students with a number of baffling discontinuities.

These discontinuities are, in ascending order of importance to modern geopolitics, the Phoenician civilization, the rise of Christianity in Imperial Rome, Iran after conquest by Alexander and finally, analysis of Indo-European culture.

The listed subjects make little sense because their history was heavily edited. The editors mainly used the cutting tool – largely, they did not have the stomach for replacing what they cut out with lies. It was the latter historians who patched holes in the fabric with threads of varying integrity.

The evolution of Christian Europe on the ruins of the Western Roman Empire would seem to be crucial to any understanding of Europe in the subsequent centuries. Yet it is no easy task to develop a coherent image about this era, presided over by the early church – even though contemporary sources exist in abundance. The textbook version of Western history seems to pass through a long, dark tunnel of some five centuries: the Roman Empire enters at one end, and the familiar Europe seems to emerge from the other, around the time of the Crusades.

From what we do know about early church leaders, their behaviour was neither pretty nor complimentary to the image of Christianity. Given that the church was in charge of keeping chronicles and teaching literacy to thirty generations of Europeans, it is not surprising that we are left with gaps, which make the ascent of Roman clergy to power incomprehensible.

Reminiscent of skulduggery documented between fathers of the faith, the early years of Bolshevism saw personalities and ideologies locked in a merciless combat for the prize of total power.

The eventual winner proceeded to erase all evidence of this struggle. Had Lenin's successors remained in power for a few more centuries, the relevant materials would be reliably gathered up and destroyed. As it was, the population was presented with a canonical history of Soviet revolution. Materials that contradicted official textbooks were secreted in archives. Historians are likely to spend another century reconstructing the Bolshevik antics – if so permitted by the leaders of their time.

Likewise, the bitter politics behind the evolution of Christianity would have been sanitized for posterity in toto – but circumstances were different. Christianity quickly spread over a vast territory of the Roman Empire and beyond.

Based in Rome and Constantinople, the ultimate winners were not in a position to inflict their will on entire Christendom, especially after state control broke down over much of the Roman domain.

Arianism (after its founder Arius, not to be confused with anything Aryan), which we now call an early heresy, was the Christian creed of many Germanic tribes. Its followers could not be ordered about, wielding some of the best military forces in the Roman world. As a result, we know rather a lot about Arianism, whose followers needed to be won over by argument, rather than by force.

Adherents of other alternative doctrines, such as Ethiopian Orthodoxy or Nestorianism, were beyond the reach of Roman authority, and others still, such as Copts and Maronites, soon found themselves governed by Muslims, who wanted no part of church politics. As a result we ended up with many versions of Christianity. Rival churches faithfully recorded the sordid behaviour of their opponents and saved it for the mirth of posterity.

To this day, the Church of the Holy Sepulchre in Jerusalem is divided into five sections, each occupied by a different Christian creed. The holy men who reside in the five corners of the building have vicious fights, which traditionally begin over the sweeping of rubbish. The Turks, who ruled Jerusalem wisely, had confiscated the keys to the front door and handed them over to a trustworthy Muslim family (which still retains this post) to dampen unseemly behaviour, an embarrassment to self-respecting worshippers of all faiths.

The missing chapters – about the first two centuries of Christianity – would have made the most entertaining reading. But after being decriminalized, the Roman church enjoyed a century of cooperation with the state. That time was used well, erasing history and replacing it with myth. As a result, our understanding of how Christianity came to such power is impaired by a number of missing pages.

Early Christians are portrayed as persecuted martyrs, executed in ways that stray into sadistic pornography. Allegedly, formal persecution began some time in the first century and continued until 311 AD – approximately 250 years in toto.

We are asked to believe that at the end of that period a reviled and derided cult became the religion of the Roman state in 391 AD, suddenly and by a single imperial decree. The same decree also made Christianity the only legally permitted religion – with, interestingly, the exception of Judaism.

Divine intervention is hinted to be involved in Constantine's assistance. With Christianity barely out of the closet, in 325 AD Constantine saw it fit to settle differences between various Christian sects by calling the Council of Nicaea, over which he presided. It is difficult to imagine why the iron-headed soldier-emperor exerted himself in this manner, if Christians were just emerging into the light, burying their martyrs and nursing the scars from judicial proceedings.

It is also hinted that divinity stepped in again – to dispose of Julian the Apostate, a promising young emperor killed in battle before he had a chance to dethrone Christianity, which he had every intention of doing.

Whilst divine manipulation is indeed the best explanation for this version of events, it is far more probable that opinion makers of the Christian community had long enmeshed themselves in power politics, much as they do to this day. The miraculous rise of Christianity is most likely a result of determined effort by at least three generations of infiltrators at all levels of Roman society.

Gibbon gleefully notes that after only eighty years since it was legalized, the church executed its first critic – a habit of which it was cured only recently. It is known that the rise of Christianity had evoked a rich body of pagan literature that ridiculed and refuted Christianity. Virtually none of these works survive.

The last century saw a rash of accidental

discoveries, which left us a substantial library of accidentally discovered early Christian texts, buried in contravention of orders to destroy them.

They indicate that Orwellian, 1984-style editing of church history began early – by the middle of the second century AD. The revisionists cared for nothing holy, distorting facts salient to our perception of Jesus, such as the role of Mary Magdalene. Whether or not she was His wife, Mary was clearly far more than a mere camp follower, as she was portrayed in the subsequent centuries.

It is worth examining whether the repulsive tales of martyrdom contain any truth. Most observers concur with Gibbon, who denounced that blood-curdling litany as fabrication of latter clerics, deranged by compulsory celibacy. Had these tales been published today, they would have attracted severe censorship, with most modern Christians preferring to be spared the details.

But Gibbon goes overboard, as he is wont to do, in admiration of Rome and contempt for Christianity. Roman ethical standards were entirely different from modern morality. Much of Roman justice would be considered "cruel and unusual" today. Romans used various methods of execution, some quite outlandish and repulsive to modern view. In an age where few lived to their fiftieth birthday, a quick hanging or a beheading didn't have enough emotional impact.

Independent sources are quite unequivocal – some Christians were executed by being forced to battle (or tied down for) wild animals in a circus, especially in the aftermath of the great fire of Rome, which Nero accused the Christians of lighting.

It may appear improbable that a daughter of a Roman patrician was punished by breast amputation for refusing to marry a socially desirable suitor. Then one comes across a modern story of a young woman packed away in a psychiatric hospital for the same offence. The head of a Roman family, at least, wielded such power lawfully.

Then we have a saint who helpfully advised the executioner to turn him over, as he was well enough cooked on one side. That story seems a little overdone, but with skill it is possible to burn someone so slowly as to prevent them from losing conscience. The saint's feedback sounds more like mockery than display of Christian humility, but it is not impossible that he was still able to perform in this vein after sustaining a deep localized burn (if thermal injury is maintained, the nerve endings die and the pain settles, death being many hours away).

No doubt many such stories were invented for consumption in later times – but savage persecution of Christians does appear to have occurred. Surviving records also show that Roman authorities soon tired of persecuting those guilty of insanity rather than treason, and a de-facto tolerance became commonplace long before persecution ceased formally.

During the underground centuries Christians nevertheless owned consecrated churches where they met on a regular basis. They already developed a sophisticated ecclesiastical *apparat*, with an effective hierarchical structure retained to the present day.

To a Russian this story makes no sense whatsoever. Like any authoritarian society, Imperial Rome possessed an impressive police force. Its ability to infiltrate undesirable organizations is amply documented in the New Testament itself.

There were secret religious cells in the Soviet Union. They generally consisted of a few trusted individuals who met in totally clandestine circumstances – abandoned buildings, forests and, less desirably, places of abode, to worship and teach their doctrine. Most of them enjoyed a brief existence before being discovered, infiltrated and savagely eliminated.

On that experience, it is quite impossible that persecuted Christians were able to survive and worship under the nose of a hostile state for two centuries, let alone build an organization with franchises throughout the empire.

The Bolshevik revolution offers a relevant analogy: an established and heavy-handed social order was upended by a small, highly motivated clique that used ideology as a political tool. Bolsheviks took power under the banner of Marxism, but their revolution amounted to little more than a vehicle for a small group of educated men. They all came from comfortable households, and they all wanted more than their talents could deliver under the old regime.

From what little we know about early Christianity, it followed a similar path. Beginning with Paul of Tarsus, the Christian movement became hijacked by power-hungry misfits, who mercilessly drove their agenda towards success. It makes sense that like Bolshevik movement, the Christian power drive would be instantly recognized as a threat to existing social order. It makes sense that Roman authorities persecuted Christians and made examples of a few with gruesome public executions.

However Christianity survived, it is surprising. The Roman state packed a much harder punch than the weak and corrupt Czarist Russia. Nevertheless, the infiltration mechanism may have been similar. For a century prior to the actual revolution, opinion makers in Russian society polarized into two groups. Traditionalist defenders of faith and throne were opposed by liberal democrats, whose eventual radicalization spawned the Bolshevik party.

This is not to say that Russian government was unaware of the rising danger or did nothing to stop it. It did both, and it did so ruthlessly. Nevertheless the Left, as it subsequently became known, was able to hide its psychopaths amongst more civil sympathizers, such as liberally inclined journalists, academics and even gentry (for instance, Count Leo Tolstoy), who were considered very much a part of the establishment despite their socialist views.

It is probable that most early Christians were not fanatics and readily sacrificed to pagan gods on demand (which discharged them from the persecutory process). The martyrs who refused were likely to have been deranged individuals who provoked authorities in a Roman equivalent of "suicide by cop".

Paul of Tarsus and Vladimir Iliyich Lenin, the eventual leader of the Russian Revolution, had much in common. Both enjoyed penning sanctimonious sermons and playing petty politics at the expense of the big picture, and both cleverly rode their ideology to self-professed leadership of their respective movements. Curiously, "he who does not work does not eat" was a favourite slogan with both. Many generations of Soviet Marxists had chanted that catchy line, not realizing that it comes from the New Testament.

Paul disappears at the end of his life, supposedly executed without any fanfare. That, somehow, seems a waste of a martyrdom opportunity. He is said to have been beheaded at the age of around sixty – a quick, merciful death, better than any a Roman of his age would expect any day from natural causes – and what? No final words of wisdom? No touching benedictions or ringing expressions of Christian forgiveness?

A sceptical observer may envisage a different cause of this sudden, low-key departure. Paul would have done well if he "turned state witness" and betrayed as many of his flock as he could. That would secure a comfortable anonymous retirement in some pleasant corner of the Roman Empire, which had many such corners.

That kind of disappearing act is more consistent with the character of a man who wrote Paul's missives. More so, he was a self-confessed traitor to his original faith. As all intelligence services know, traitors cannot be trusted. Their information can be used as a starting point for investigation, but every word they utter must be verified from other sources.

Lenin was spirited out of Russia and comfortably housed in Zurich by German intelligence (Germany being at war with Russia at the time). He was later returned in a special "sealed" train that sped him to Sweden through Germany. Like most German trains, it arrived precisely on time, depositing Lenin in the middle of a power vacuum. A venomous reptile was nurtured in a cage until a master assassin tossed its scaly length into the bed of his victim.

Today, more than ever, the good men and women who believe in Jesus of Nazareth deserve the truth about their antecedents. The long-term future of their faith depends on an honest reappraisal free of propaganda sculpted to appease the Roman authorities. The Roman Empire, after all, is no longer in charge.

It is pertinent to contrast the history of early Christianity to the treatment of Carthage, another great defect in the conventional perception of history. That early enemy of the West nearly succeeded in becoming the dominant global culture. But after annihilation of Roman forces at Cannae, Hannibal hesitated and failed to attack the city of Rome, calculating that his political sponsors will not have the stomach to support such upheaval in the contemporary world order. But for that, my text may have been written from right to left in a Semitic script used by the Punic civilization.

Most known sources that mention Carthage were penned by her bitter enemies, Greeks and Romans. A little more can be derived from the studies in the original homeland of Carthaginians (modern Lebanon) and subsequent colonies in the Mediterranean.

It cannot be said that Carthage is neglected by archaeologists – today her remains are being slowly but surely unearthed by a large army of investigators. Yet our understanding of daily life in ancient Carthage remains nebulous.

The main reason for this is not in dispute – Rome vowed to erase Carthage, and her legionaries faithfully carried out that promise. The troops were ordered to preserve a certain written work, a comprehensive treatise on agriculture, and that text, lost in toto but surviving in fragmented translation, is the only Carthaginian book that survived at all.

Carthaginians were not the poor writers they are portrayed today. Rather, their libraries were handed over to Numidia, their neighbour who sided with Romans (territory of present Algeria). Numidia enjoyed a chequered history after Roman rule collapsed in Africa, and Carthaginian libraries failed to survive.

As a sample of what they offered, the Phoenicians invented the phonetic alphabet. Alpha and beta are not Greek words: *aleph* (alpha), the first letter of the Phoenician alphabet, meant "bull", just as it does in modern Hebrew. *Ba-it* (beta) meant "house", *gimel* (gamma) – "camel". The sounds with which these words began were represented by characters that resembled the respective objects.

We have a lot of second-hand information about Carthage. Romans writers devoted it much attention, and they did not ridicule an enemy that nearly achieved their demise. To do so would insult the titanic Roman effort that went into winning that savage contest. They understood this well and had no difficulty in describing Carthage as a military, political and commercial heavyweight, which it undoubtedly was.

The Roman sources hasten to add that Carthaginians were vicious, cruel, perfidious and barbarous. For some reason modern historians labour to refute these assertions, although they can be nothing but self-evident truths. Like all empires that play for keeps, the Carthaginian state must have dispensed perfidy and barbarism in abundance. It is more pertinent and relevant to suggest that Rome did the same – self-evidently excelling Carthage in these pursuits.

Conventional historians don't seem to be in a hurry to fill in the gaps. Modern textbooks faithfully reproduce Greek and Roman view of the conflict without any attempt at balance. The Roman struggle against Carthage is portrayed in black and white terms, akin to the war against Nazism in Europe. By implication, the evil, cruel Carthaginians could not have won.

Alas, the facts themselves indicate that Roman

victory was a near-run thing. There is no obvious reason why Rome should have succeeded – it came down to particulars of numerous circumstances and personalities in a wide-ranging conflict. All assertions to the contrary boil down to a supremacist stereotyping of Rome, the standard bearer of Western civilization, versus the barbarous hordes of Semitic Carthage, guilty of breaking oaths and offering human sacrifice.

Many are surprised to learn that during the Second Punic War Rome was also barbarous enough to offer human sacrifice – shortly after the disaster at Cannae – and that Carthage was a republic like Rome, but with many more centuries of culture at its back.

Undoubtedly, however, modern civilization is heavily indebted to Carthage, an ancient culture that fought Greeks for control of Mediterranean for a better part of a millennium.

Above: coin showing Hannibal's image. Below: a bust of Hannibal

A drawing of the only Carthaginian building found intact –
a mausoleum built for a Lybian chieftain by a
Carthaginian architect. It was tipped on its side intact and
preserved in the ground near the town of Sabratha.

Its use of traditional Ionic elements in this totally novel
manner is an evocative illustration of what Carthaginian
civilization could have offered humanity.

Given the treatment of Carthage, it is not surprising that conventional teaching offers little more than confusion about Iran, whose civilization is quite alive, if not very well, today.

According to Western textbooks, Iranians simply disappear after Alexander. A millennium of ground-breaking and glorious culture is reduced to footnotes, lest we confuse our world view with facts. Most innovations that came from Iran tend to be passed off as salient features of European culture. Yet imagining Western civilization devoid of Iranian input is a humbling exercise indeed.

A special oblivion is constructed for Iran's greatest gift to the world – the ethical system of Zarathushtra. Whilst reading the compact body of works that is Western literature about Iran, one need only blink to miss the mention of Zoroastrianism altogether.

Iran's greatest archaeological treasures lie in the earth possessed by a vicious totalitarian regime – one that has reason to misrepresent the origins of Iranian culture. Ancient scholarship lies even more neglected than monuments, with most historians giving the Zoroastrian creed a wide berth.

That seems strange. It is simply impossible to write about European history without extensive reference to Christianity, which dominated

European culture for sixteen centuries. The same applies to the Islamic world, and it would be simply ridiculous to ignore Judaism in any study of Jewish history.

But as with Carthage, Iran's history is largely written by Western antagonists. The last sources to speak of Iranians with respect are the likes of Herodotus, himself an ethnic Greek and a subject of Persia from a Greek colony in Asia Minor.

Western sources are almost religious in their adherence to the image of violent barbarians when they come to describe Iran, beginning with the Greek wars. Even in more enlightened modern times, Iranians have vexed European prejudice to the full.

On one hand they had succumbed to the Greek arms, which allegedly proves their civilization to be inferior. Yet no one suggests that Nazi Germany boasted a civilization superior to that of democratic France, whose feeble attempts at resistance Germany crushed with ease. The sophisticated French culture had to be rescued – again – by Americans with barbaric accents and the British, whose barbaric cuisine remains a running insult to French sensibilities.

Iranians began the war with Greece and are thus considered anti-Western – anti-us. We believe Byron, who said "We are all Greeks", do we not? Yet Rome also attacked and annexed Greece, but no one accuses Romans of being anti-Western. Heaven, Rome *is* the West – even if you believe that we have progressed, modern European and American cultures still rest on a Roman foundation.

Ah, but Iranians are Asian. Now we are getting somewhere, says the Western bigot – Asiatics are inferior to Europeans. This is what a British scholar of Parthian history had to say about Asians:

"Their sculptures give them the large, ill-formed limbs, the heavy paunches, and the general flaccid appearance which characterises the Turanian [Turkic] races. Their history shows them to have had the merits and the defects of the Turanian type of character. They were covetous, grasping, ready to take the aggressive, and on the whole, tolerably successful in their wars against weak races. But they were wanting in dash, vigorous effort and perseverance. They were stronger in defence than in attack; and, as time went on, became more and more unenterprising and lethargic."

George Rawlinson, "Parthia", 1893

Except, and much to the chagrin of stereotype-mongers, Iranians are Caucasians – rather large and handsome Caucasians at that. They are not at all the degenerate üntermenschen we seek for an embodiment of prejudice.

Later in this book the reader will have an opportunity to examine some examples of Parthian art and decide whether it is characterized by "flaccid appearance". As for the

Parthians themselves, their enemies do not appear to have judged them as lacking either perseverance or vigour.

Indeed, the white supremacist is in for a disappointment – Aryan stock belongs more to Asia than Europe (not to mention that the entire construct of Asia owes more to racism than geography).

It is much easier to distance Iranians from modern Europeans on the basis of Islam – except that far from all Iranians are Muslim, even officially. Many more call themselves Muslims because it is not safe to do otherwise.

Between all these prejudices, the influence of a profoundly important culture is reduced to a subliminal undercurrent in our perception.

In reality, Iran has retained its established and highly developed culture all the way to modern times. It did not have the Greek flair for art and philosophy (and neither did anyone else apart from Greeks) – but it is utterly impossible to dismiss the Iranian contribution to human progress.

That contribution begins at the dawn of recorded history, when Zarathushtra laid the foundation of an integrated ethical system. Most of the world takes such a system for granted today.

"We" of today's West are not Greeks. They gave

us the foundation of our arts and they founded the Western tradition of scientific method. They did not give us a foundation of our ethics, either individual or collective.

Whatever may be said of the arts, the scientific method is worthless without such ethics – as it was worthless in the hands of the Greeks, who did not have the integrity to develop it into modern science.

The Greek engineers, mathematicians and physicians had access to the same technology as the great thinkers of the Renaissance – but they failed to understand circulation, harness steam or conceptualize Newtonian mechanics.

Those advances awaited a very different set of attitudes, beginning with a commitment to the truth. The Greeks preferred conceptual elegance over rude reality. Consequently, were not rigorous practitioners of the scientific method, their scientific theories having to compete with witty myths.

"We" are mainly Germanic, Slavonic and Celtic nations. "Our" legislative framework is Germanic and Roman. "Our" ethical system comes from a Semitic culture that itself heavily borrowed from Iranian Zoroastrianism. The Semitic ethical system was itself modified along European lines – as a Jewish sect, the Christians got nowhere fast. But when they restyled

Christianity to suit the Roman mindset, it soon gained control of the Roman world and beyond.

Christianity has partially retraced its steps to a Judaic origin during Reformation. But even as a reformed creed, it still carries the legacy of being a tool of social control in the service of a steel-fisted empire.

But the most damaging hiatus in the understanding of our Western "we" is rooted in prehistory. Central to the subject of this book, it is the sorry state of scholarship about the origins of Indo-European culture – and the reasons for its indisputable success.

The Indo-European phenomenon is of towering significance to global history, and little in history can be understood outside that context. The reasons for such success deserve intricate study: three out of four modern humans speak an Indo-European language from birth. The influence of Indo-European cultures (Latin, Germanic, Indian and Slavonic) speaks for itself in geopolitical terms.

Only two cultural blocs – Chinese centred on South-East Asia and Semitic, centred on Northern Africa, speak non-Indo-European languages and practise cultures that are quite distinct from that of Indo-Europeans.

The origin of Indo-European culture is usually glossed over because of its well-advertised brutality. It takes much trawling through scholarly texts to gain even a modicum of a feel for this culture, even though its features still characterize most Indo-European societies.

This failure to connect the dots is a sad outcome of political correctness. It is very costly failure, which deprives us of our greatest treasure – the definition of our identity.

This is no mere academic consideration. I find history more practical than chemistry or physics, disciplines of which I have good working knowledge. History is always the missing ingredient whenever a major geopolitical error is made. In modern times ignorance results in strategic errors by leaders who command vast armies and nuclear arsenals. Gaps that make history difficult to interpret are more of an impediment to progress than was once a belief that the sun travels around the earth.

An aesthetic distaste for the violent and inhumane aspects of their legacy has led modern Indo-Europeans to contort themselves into impractical and unviable structures such as Marxism. Every such attempt has made Indo-European excesses worse.

Even worse consequences arose from an opposite movement, which glorified the worst of what Indo-European culture has to offer. This endeavour awakened a true monstrosity – the fascist state, a malignant entity that thrives on war and subrogation of individual rights.

Failure to understand what shaped the Western civilisation also leads into fatal error those who attack it. Even a cursory study of the path travelled by Indo-Europeans shows, with utter certainty, the futility of Islamic fanaticism.

Most commentators agree that for the past century Western society is suffering from a number of degenerative trends, whose sum total may be described as an evolving crisis. This crisis can be seen as a collective failure of social models tried out by Indo-Europeans as alternatives to their innate culture – religions, Marxism, fascism, Neo-Paganism and even the vacant modern creed of nihilistic consumerism.

There appears to be no obvious way forward. There is no way back, either: resurgence of primaeval Indo-European culture along the lines of ancient Rome or Nazi Germany is not an option in the thermonuclear age.

In that context, we turn to a creed now covered with the rubble of failed ideas and hypocrisy. Its ideas have run through Western civilization as powerful undercurrents – one can only wonder what would happen if they ran explicitly.

Introduction to Zoroastrianism

It is quite striking how few even know of Zoroastrian faith today. Yet it underlies a stupendous amount of our heritage; modern world would not be recognizable without the concepts first enunciated by a minor aristocrat in Central Asia.

This turning point in evolution of humanity occurred earlier than originally thought; it is now considered that Zarathushtra lived between 1500 to 1700 BC. Initially Western scholars who rediscovered his religion in late nineteenth century placed him near the time of Cyrus – sixth century BC – but recent linguistic analysis of Zoroastrian texts strongly suggests a date at least a millennium earlier.

The Greeks called him Zoroaster, possibly distorting the original name to give it meaning in their language, for they respected him greatly. "Zoë" is life, "astra" is star – Star of Life, not an inappropriate epithet for the author of his ideas.

The name is conventionally translated as something like a camel herder or a possessor of yellow camels, meaning, possibly, a prized breed. However, that has recently been challenged to suggest that "Zarathushtra" refers to the star of Sirius, as the Greeks indeed implied.

From what we are handed down, Zarathushtra came from a well-to-do family in Bactria, somewhere in the territory of modern Tajikistan or Afghanistan. The story of his life has an authentic ring – seeking the protection of wealthy patrons from violent retribution by adherents of the old religion he sought to replace. One tradition says that the said adherents caught up with him, killing him at prayer at a very advanced age of 77.

Reassurance can be found in the relative lack of embellishment of his person in the Zoroastrian canon. Other than in predictable folk tales, Zarathushtra is portrayed as a wise, humble man who is otherwise in no way unworldly. Unlike Jesus he performed no miracles. Unlike Mohammed he did not tour heaven before death. He is not to be worshipped in any manner. The descendants of his issue have disappeared without trace, and the only thing that makes him special is that he was chosen to transmit a revelation – an obligation he may be considered to have discharged in full.

Recent analysis showed that the language of Gathas, hymns Zarathushtra is said to have composed in person, is much older than the language prevalent at the time of Cyrus. In both language and content there is a strong similarity between the Gathas and the sacred Hindu library of Rig Veda, conventionally dated from early second millennium BC. Furthermore, Ahura Mazda ("Wise Lord", the God of Zarathushtra) is mentioned in the Assyrian archives dated to eighth century BC. These developments allow the once-supreme hypothesis – that Zarathushtra living around the same time as Cyrus the Great – to be safely discarded safely.

Then I said to it first: I am Zarathushtra. I am, as far as I can be, a true opponent of the wrong and a strong ally of the right.

(Gathas: viii)

Gathas suggest that Zarathushtra came from a smaller settlement somewhere in Bactria (modern Tajikistan), later moving to what we know as the Afghan city of Balkh. According to other sources, he lived in Herat (which remains a population centre in modern Afghanistan) – but there is a definite convergence of locations to one region.

His ethnicity is squarely Indo-European, of Indo-Iranian delineation. In Zarathushtra's day Iranian tribes occupied most of modern Southern Russia, Ukraine, Central Asia, Southern Siberia as well as modern Iran and eastern Iraq.

Zarathushtra's society was in the throes of a transition, stone tools being replaced with metal. That triggered rapid changes with major social implications – politically, it was a world in constant flux and chaos. Its citizens led a precarious existence under constant threat from climate and fellow humans. Widespread use of writing lay in a distant future, and travel was a slow, haphazard activity, making whatever there was for a government a nominal entity, for it could only rule by direct force over a small area within the radius of practicable communication. In essence, government only existed wherever the local ruler could get to with his soldiers (and where he was able to feed them) at any given time.

That environment exhibits surprising parallels to what many find today: whilst we fear neither sword nor famine, our livelihood must be constantly defended against merciless enemies of an endemic nature – large entities, public and private, that trample on rights and means of individual survival.

Central authority is again absent from this struggle – barely present in Zarathushtra's time, today it is diluted by red tape to the point of irrelevance – or sold to the highest bidder. Although we believe that we enjoy full protection of the law, in practice such safety is only the province of the few, whose power is not so much comprised of dollars as effective use of political means.

Today's causes are won by manipulating public emotions rather than by ancient instruments of blade and fire. But, as in Zarathushtra's time, wars are won by having better weapons and better motivated combatants.

The crux of Zarathushtra's achievement lies in recognition that human society is an ecosystem within a wider ecology from which it derives its survival. Both systems and their interactions are subject to a set of ecological principles, and if these principles are deviated from, society becomes less viable and can become extinct altogether.

We take this for granted today, but it was Zarathushtra who delineated this concept. Yet layers of civilization that insulate us from the harsh prehistoric reality can prove illusory and transient – as Romans who survived the collapse of the Western Empire eloquently attested.

By dividing the universe between poles of good and evil, Zarathushtra constructed an all-encompassing concept of morality, an ethical equivalent of what physicists call the unified field theory. Far from an arbitrary and simplistic "Axis of Evil" classification we are exhorted to enhance today, Zarathushtra's system is an objective algorithm, applicable not only to human interactions, but also to a wider relationship between humanity and its environment.

Zarathushtra saw evil not only in damaging or destructive actions towards fellow citizens, but also in sloth and disorder. He fused into one conceptual framework the concepts of law, citizenship and utilitarianism – an acceptance that humans require productivity as a backbone to their self-esteem. A recognition that murder, theft, laziness and untidiness are related phenomena on the same sliding scale was not only revolutionary for his time but remains so today.

To restate: lack of hygiene, failure to maintain aesthetic surroundings and destructive land management are all evil, only quantitatively different to homicide or theft. Modern concepts of chaos theory and second law of thermodynamics, of vital relevance to all biological systems, are little more than scientific expressions of the same concept, which ancient Indo-Iranians called Asha – a term signifying a natural order, an ecological equilibrium in modern parlance.

To him who, through the good mind, performs his duties in thoughts, words, and deeds in accordance with what is right, the Wise God grants completeness and immortality, through security and serenity.

(Gathas: xii)

Zarathushtra was born into a river oasis society of Central Asia. His culture represented the first stage of permanent Indo-European settlement in that terrain, surviving through dry farming (without artificial irrigation). Most Indo-

European immigrants made a transition to permanent settlement, as abandonment of ancestral nomadic ways of their native grassland was dictated by new terrain. But some continued to rove, becoming bands of robbers who preyed on farming settlers.

There was a powerful symbolic contrast to this choice of careers – a subsistence life of a farmer or that of a predator, living off those who make their living sustainably.

I ask to know: how does a settler, by his decent actions, strengthen the world with righteousness? He is a humble thinker who is a true leader of the law-abiding and is seen as the ruler of the blessed.

(Gathas: xvi)

Zarathushtra's world saw a rapid escalation of violence. Bronze Age technology was now widespread, yielding weapons of unprecedented effectiveness, and light chariots were perfected around the same time. The arrival of the chariot and metal weapons exacerbated the divide between the farmer and the aggressor.

The content of the Gatha texts suggest that Zarathushtra witnessed the effect of that divide first-hand. The anguish of his descriptions makes it clear that he witnessed this enhanced Darwinism in action, perhaps barely surviving its effects.

To envisage Zarathushtra's world one must

imagine a sandy and rocky plain that is generally treeless and waterless, except along rivers that run from nearby mountains. Belts of dense vegetation grow along riverbanks, where alluvial soil is kept fertile the by rich mineral content of snow-fed mountain streams.

Dry farming (as opposed to the latter system of canal irrigation) consisted of clearing the natural waterside vegetation to grow crops in the vicinity of the stream. Settlements that date from the third millennium BC onwards appear as small multi-room riverside fortresses of mud brick, presumably occupied by an extended family and its livestock. The extent of fortification implied a danger of precisely the kind described in the Gathas: raids by small bands of bandit clans – small because larger forces would easily overwhelm a typical river fort.

There is little reason to presume that the climate of Central Asia is different today. Unlike, for instance, North Africa, there are no remains of ancient agricultural practices that indicate a more favourable environment in previous times.

Survival of settlers at the dawn of Bronze Age differed little from how Afghans live today – bone-chilling winters in a terrain with little fuel, blazing summers in which the life-giving rivers dry up with little warning, barren soil that sustains only a small population (ancient river forts are spaced a constant number of miles apart). It is a life of poor diet, difficult sanitation and constant threat of attack, in which ferocity, surprise and numbers were the sole determinants of outcome.

The Soul of the Living World lamented to You: why did You create me? Who made me this way? I am oppressed by fury, rapine, injustice and carnage. I have no one to restore me other than You. Lead me to a true society.

Righteousness replied: there is no ruler in the world who is free from malice. Of those below I know none who would induce the strong to help the weak. Had there been one man strong enough among them, I would have hurried to his call.

(Gathas: i – iii)

The derivation of Zarathushtra's values is thus simple to reconstruct. Procreation is encouraged, for superior numbers mean survival. Any practices that distract from or interfere with reproduction are abhorred. Productivity is of paramount importance, as food supply is sparse and unreliable.

Environmental sustainability is all, since building a river fort is a major investment in a permanent location, which must be kept sanitary and agriculturally sustainable for generations to come. In particular, excrement and infectious waste must be disposed of meticulously and with much forethought, as it is amongst such farmers today.

Pollution of fundamental elements of Iranian ethos – fire, water, earth, sun and metal – is expressly forbidden. Hence the Zoroastrian practice of not burying or cremating the dead, but leaving them for vultures and other predators away from the settlement, usually on a waterless hilltop in specially built enclosures aptly named "towers of silence". Soil farmed with primitive implements (long-handed stone axes, sticks and the odd animal bone – the Russian word for the shoulder blade is still the diminutive form of "shovel") was too precious, and digging a suitable deep grave, especially in winter, is too great an effort without good tools.

We know that in earlier times Indo-Europeans buried their dead in earth mounds, but that was a practice of a people constantly moving around in a grass sea. Those who came south to modern Afghanistan and beyond had to make many adjustments after leaving the foothills of the Urals abundant with food and water – which latter Aryan folklore correctly represents as paradise itself.

From a fort dweller's point of view, it was not difficult to classify every occupant of the landscape as good or evil. Survival tends to focus one's outlook on the "friend or foe" question.

That long-term survival lay in a sustainable but difficult life was self-evident, as was the fact that pillage was the main enemy of sustainable life –

and without farmers there was no survival for either.

Those who produced signified the good, and those who destroyed were evidently evil. Dogs and cattle were good beasts. Snakes and wolves were not – the logic of which is self-evident. The cat made it into bad books, for this was not a society possessed of large granaries that make control of rodents a vital endeavour; at that time and place cats were wild predators, nothing but a threat to livestock.

Zarathushtra exhorted people to take pleasure in life. Not for him the gloomy sadomasochism of European attitudes to sex and other natural pleasures. Zoroastrians are required to behave modestly in public, but not for them the denigration of women, which reaches dismal lows in Abrahamic religions (Judaism, Christianity and Islam). Mediaeval Christianity is responsible for amazing feats of misogyny, labelling women as vessels of Satan.

Modern Christian, Muslim and Jewish opinion makers are left to wrestle with antediluvian attitudes of their predecessors to numerous aspects of gender inequality, in resolution of which I wish them luck and speed. In contrast, Zoroastrians do not believe that Satan glued genitals onto God's creation. One is encouraged to have a sex life (although Zoroastrians never accepted homosexual activity, in theory at least)

There is no sin in wine either – in fact, ancient Iranians were reported to have taken that freedom to its outer limit. They had a curious custom, according to Herodotus, of making all important decisions whilst drunk and then reviewing them once sober – a somewhat unusual brainstorming technique, but, no doubt, one they used to advantage. Alcohol does sometimes enhance creativity – if nothing else, by lowering inhibitions that prevent less extrovert of thinkers from sharing their thoughts.

But not so keen was Zarathushtra on a psychoactive substance pertaining to the old Iranian religion, haoma (sometimes transliterated as soma). There is still a dispute about its active ingredients, but the consensus is that it was probably a stimulant extracted from the ephedra plant, a forerunner of modern pseudoephedrine (which is a synthetic form of ephedra's main ingredient). Judging by some of the descriptions, the drug was combined with other agents, such as cannabis or opium. More likely than not, the recipe varied with the region and available resources.

Ritual use of ephedra is associated with many early Indo-European cultures. It is also known from Hindu sources, and sticks of ephedra are found in Tocharian graves of the Tarim Basin (vide infra). Consumption of mind-altering substances as a shamanistic ritual has equivalents in many other cultures. The priest, or the entire congregation, consumes a hallucinogen. The resultant effects are used to seek portents for the future, to communing with a deity and to remove social inhibitions. The modern "speaking in tongues" phenomenon is a similar practice, in which altered mental state is achieved through self-hypnosis (or, as some would label it, induction of mass hysteria).

When shall they throw out the filthy poison? It is through that poison that priests and wicked rulers of the lands form their evil minds.

(Gathas: xiii)

Haoma seems to be associated with the priestly establishment, which Zarathushtra severely denounced. He accused the priests of the old religion of corruption, hypocrisy and other common failings of an ecclesiastical establishment:

The mumbling priests are not friends. They are sufficiently far from laws and from the settlement. They take delight in injuring the world with their deeds and teachings, a thinking that ultimately places them in the house of wrong.

(Gathas: xvi)

It is even possible that the mumbling priests held a monopoly on haoma manufacture (by keeping its composition secret). That would have been a curious arrangement – consider the dynamics that would result from the church having an alcohol monopoly in Russia or France.

Hallucinogens frequently produce scenes that sober and sober-minded observers find ugly. But it appears as if Zarathushtra was attacking more than a profitable monopoly or an unpleasant religious practice. It is no coincidence that Indra – the Indo-Iranian god of bad masculinity – was demoted, along with his cohorts of daevas (formerly equivalents of angels), to demonic status by Zarathushtra's reforms.

The orgiastic religious practices were hard to dissociate from the glorified violence perpetrated by Indra's earthly imitators. A modern observer is equally familiar with drunken orgies of cutthroats, whose thuggery is celebrated, justified and encouraged in revelry that is not at all merry. That was the culture of nomadic robber barons, who alternated between engorgement and rapine.

Zoroastrianism singled out one human failing with particular vehemence. Those who lie, said Zarathushtra, are making straight for the devil.

According to Herodotus:

Their sons are carefully instructed from their fifth to their twentieth year, in three things alone, – to ride, to draw the bow, and to speak the truth.

The Greeks were amazed by this aspect of Iranian culture – children were brought up not to lie under any circumstances. Greeks themselves enjoyed deceiving their opponents as much as they enjoyed outrunning or out-shooting them in sporting events. A refusal to lie must have struck them as an exemplary barbarian failure to appreciate what life has to offer.

Specifically, righteous and productive people are a delight to Zarathushtra's God. They have no reason to demean themselves on the account of original sin, abase themselves or belittle their achievements – a direct antithesis of the Christian and Muslim doctrines.

In Zoroastrianism a human being is an agent of Divinity, endowed with his immense powers for a reason. People are not miserable and detestable sinners who must submit or beg for redemption – they are instead rational, independent beings who have the wherewithal to make the obligatory choice between good and evil. That choice cannot be influenced from above – but there are consequences, whatever path one chooses.

With such actions evil doers fall victim to deception and derision. Let them all scream on their behalf. Let, by means of good ruler, the killing and maiming be stopped and [let] peace be brought to homes and settlements. Let diseases disappear. Greatest is one who restrains killing.

(Gathas: xvii)

It is not a graduated choice, for the moral universe is a battleground between good and evil. Whichever side one chooses, there is no selectivity of action. You cannot consider yourself good because you refrain from murder whilst being a thief or a liar. Zarathushtra's God wants those who believe in the principle, leaving those with selective moral purity to the Adversary.

In so structuring his view of the universe, Zarathushtra avoids three landmines that plagued Abrahamic religions since the beginning: the doctrines of omnipotence, omniscience and prescience.

The Yahweh of Moses is everywhere, as is Ahura Mazda of Zarathushtra. But Yahweh knows everything in advance because nothing happens without His will. In contrast, Zarathushtra's God does not interfere with free will of any sentient being, and, accordingly, the choice between good and evil is made by any given individual, without being predestined to choose one way or another.

Therefore, Ahura Mazda is neither omnipotent nor omniscient. This may strike us as alien to the concept of monotheism, but that is only our preconception.

Modern Zoroastrians insist that the ins and outs of their religion can be reduced to a simple statement: "Good Thoughts, Good Words, Good

Deeds". It is a creed of optimism – good will triumph, and negativity does nothing but reduce morale in what is, after all, a cosmic war.

In short, Zarathushtra made two monumental leaps in theology, which brought religion out of Bronze Age into the twenty-first century. Not only was one God elevated into a position of supremacy over other divine beings – but that God now required an adherence to a moral code.

Today it is difficult to describe what advance the latter represented.

Generally, the gods of early societies cared not a whit for morality. They required ritual and worship, certainly respect and fear – but not adherence to a code of conduct. Even a cursory inspection of Greek myths shows that concepts such as natural justice or due process were entirely foreign to Greek religion. Greek gods freely practise murder, rape and bestiality, and they deceive each other at every opportunity, mostly for sport. In the vicious Olympian board game humans are insignificant and expendable pawns. Sometimes, a man with sheer pluck can barter a successful passage through that board, but the general attitude of Greek gods towards mortals can be described as sadistic contempt. This is representative of all early religions, whose mythology reflected the brutal reality in which their worshippers lived harsh and brief lives.

Egyptian god Seth murders another god Osiris, but this does not at all diminish his divinity: Seth was worshipped because he is feared, and his worship aims to appease him into refraining from further amusements at human expense. He is neither loved nor does he inspire – but that is of no concern to Seth.

In latter stages of their evolution all religions place an increasing stress on a connection between personal righteousness and divine displeasure. It is difficult for a religion to survive unless it threatens divine condemnation for socially destructive acts. But that is a natural progression of a social system that strives to be less wasteful and more stable, and such maturation requires centuries.

In contrast, Zoroastrian observance was linked to moral behaviour at the outset – a revolutionary development at such an early age.

Zarathushtra did away with sacrifice, reducing the altar to a platform for a sacred flame – a much more aesthetic focus of worship and meditation. The sacred fire of Zoroastrianism represents the Sun. It is not to be contaminated with anything like animal flesh.

All ancient societies used sacrifice as a main channel of communicating with their gods. At one end of the spectrum there were relatively non-destructive practices such as sacred prostitution, abstinence from work during festive occasions and offerings of food as sacrifice. At the other end of the spectrum we have the religions of Pre-Columbian Americans, who believed that gods require human sacrifice to maintain natural phenomena such as sunshine and rain.

Baal, the main Phoenician god, had a taste for child sacrifice. Sacrificial offerings to Baal did not, contrary to naïve bleating of three generations of modern archaeologists, amount to cremation of children already deceased from natural causes. Nor were they ritualized mercy killings of children who were ill or otherwise physically inferior.

No. According to recent archaeological findings, Phoenicians sacrificed young boys who were entirely healthy.

Parents who surrendered first-born sons to have throats cut and thrown into the flames in their presence had to wear terracotta masks with what we today call a sardonic grin – to hide their grief from the god, for such grief would invalidate their sacrifice. These grotesque masks are found in abundance in all remains of Phoenician settlements, and the very term "sardonic" refers to their profusion on the island of Sardinia, once a large Phoenician colony.

In modern society there are many parents,

separated from their children by a pagan legal system devoid of common sense and contemptuous of children and their rights. There is not the slightest suggestion that parents excluded from the lives of their children somehow deserve it. The motivation for this separation is usually economic, the child being a pawn in the financial war between estranged parents. Dollars are the reward for the child sacrifice to a modern Baal.

Many parents who lose their children in this manner proceed to throw away their social position and other aspects of their citizenship. Upon the loss of their assets they cease practising their professions and live on the fringe, making a minimal income or milking the welfare system. Many move to far-off destinations where their labour can no longer be plundered by the ex-spouse.

Being so sacrificed on the altar of political correctness leaves the victims with a devastating scar on their psyche. They have not a trace of original respect for their society. They despise its entire judicial system and come to abhor its moral foundation.

It is hard to even begin to contemplate the damage done to Phoenician society through its practice of cutting children's throats in the presence of their parents.

By forming a concept of religious observance through moral behaviour rather than sacrifice of valuable resources, let alone human beings, Zarathushtra had removed a heavy overhead that no ancient society could truly afford. This bold move improved the viability of society in many ways.

Linkage of religion with observance of ethical principles in lieu of destructive sacrifice constituted a massive advance in social progress, far more so than the discovery of the atom. Indeed, the latter event is a relatively minor consequence of the former. Society would simply not be able to develop to that point of sophistication had it continued to devour itself.

Zarathushtra did not manage to do away with the priesthood – throughout the recorded history of Zoroastrian Iran there was an uneasy relationship between priests and mainstream Zoroastrians. It is poignant that Zarathushtra went to such lengths to denounce priestly intermediaries, and trouble arrived as soon as his advice was disregarded.

The Magi, from whom the modern word "magic" derives, appear in the record around the time of Cyrus. They were a secretive priestly caste, possibly an entirely separate Iranian tribe, as portrayed by Herodotus.

They probably pre-dated Zarathushtra, being the

very priests he denounced. If so, they would have fought his creed unsuccessfully, as portrayed in the Gathas, but jumped on the bandwagon when Zoroastrianism became popular – blending the traditional, pre-Zoroastrian elements of worship with his doctrine.

After the death of Cyrus they even attempted a priestly coup d'état, which Darius eventually defeated. It is curious whether his subsequent endorsement of Zoroastrian fundamentalism (the practice of religion without an ecclesiastic hierarchy) was related to his early experiences with priestly machinations.

Zoroastrian priesthood returned with a vengeance in latter times, and its revival resulted in a severe setback to the development of the Zoroastrian ethical system. The culmination of the priestly ascendancy in latter times was a racket that paralleled the worst excesses of the Vatican. It even diluted the Zoroastrian monotheism with a revival of pagan deities, although not quite as shamelessly as in Europe, where local traditions of pagan worship were thinly disguised as cults of various saints.

This departure from Zarathushtra's central idea resulted in damaging consequences – if for no other reason, then the following. When Arabs conquered Iran, the Zoroastrian population faced a stark choice – remain true or convert to Islam. Alas, their religion was heavily tainted by the political machinations of Zoroastrian clergy and marred by departure from monotheism, and that made it easier for many Zoroastrians to be convinced that Islam is merely a different name for what their religion stood for all along.

A cardinal source of Islam's political strength is its prohibition of ecclesiastic establishment – God is worshipped with no intermediaries. There is no such thing as a Muslim priest – the Imam is chosen by the local community, and his qualification for the job is scholarship, rather than graduation through a specific hierarchy, as is the case in the Catholic and Orthodox churches.

An immense amount of corruption and machination results from having a religious state within a state, which exists in an uneasy relationship with secular government. Naked political ambitions of the early fathers of Christianity had often resulted in a paralysis of secular authority – setbacks the struggling empire could ill afford.

Today Zoroastrians still worship in fire temples – easily recognizable structures built around a sacred flame. The fires burning in these temples are sacred symbols of Ahura Mazda, not to be contaminated with human breath.

There is again a priestly establishment in Zoroastrianism – this time low-key, but only so because modern Zoroastrians have survived as enclaves in societies either indifferent or hostile to their religion.

Even so, the modern priestly establishment manages to affect a negative outcome, by closing Zoroastrian communities to new converts. In a modern world that seems particularly senseless, even if Zoroastrianism has never been a proselytizing religion – most Zoroastrian communities have been isolated for many generations and could well do with new blood.

Alas, free-spirited people who choose to leave their former religion for Zoroastrianism may be harder to browbeat. Such people may be less tolerant of the priest's personal and professional failings and may feel free to cut him down to size, rather than kneel at his feet.

The creed that Zarathushtra reformed was a polytheism classic of early Indo-European societies. Retained references to the old Iranian religion make it sound very similar to ancient Hinduism. Like Moses (who probably was an historical figure), Zarathushtra condensed the pantheon of existing deities, good and bad, placing a supreme God as an overlord of six other divine beings. He also placed an evil godhead of lesser supremacy as an overlord of all that is evil, also personified by six semi-divine figures.

This is how Herodotus (? 480 BC – ? 425 BC) reports on the religion of contemporary Persians:

The customs which I know the Persians to observe are the following: they have no images of the gods, no temples nor altars, and consider the use of them a sign of folly. This comes, I think, from their not believing the gods to have the same nature with men, as the Greeks imagine.

Their wont, however, is to ascend the summits of the loftiest mountains, and there to offer sacrifice to Jupiter, which is the name they give to the whole circuit of the firmament. They likewise offer to the sun and moon, to the earth, to fire, to water, and to the winds. These are the only gods whose worship has come down to them from ancient times. At a later period they began the worship of Urania, which they borrowed from the Arabians and Assyrians. Mylitta is the name by which the Assyrians know this goddess, whom the Arabians call Alitta, and the Persians Mitra.

The female goddess became known in Sassanid times as Anahita. Mithra, the god of the victory, became a sub-deity in Zoroastrian pantheon, to be transformed into an Archangel Michael-style figure. Mazda, the god of creation, became the supreme deity.

All that seems to have little to do with Zoroastrianism as we understand it. But it is unlikely that Herodotus was wrong on such a fundamental point. He was, after all, a native of the Persian Empire, and had Zoroastrianism in its pure form been the sole religion of the masses, that would have earned much attention on Herodotus' part.

It appears that strict Zoroastrianism was a

religion of the ruling elite and possibly enclaves such as Bactria, where Zarathushtra is said to have converted the local royal family and spent most of his latter life – Bactrians regarded themselves as champions of Zoroastrianism, as many of their descendants do to this day. The rest of Iranians may have remained true to the older, more accessible pagan religion with its primitive rites, the Magi weaving self-seeking webs between the two camps.

An analogous situation arose in Europe, remaining centuries after official conversion to Christianity. Old pagan practices, superstitions, customs and festivals were banished from palaces but continued to be adhered to by rural population (the term "pagan" comes from the Latin *pagus,* meaning rural or rustic). Indeed, the two main holidays of the Christian calendar – Easter and Christmas – are pagan festivals of spring and winter solstice respectively, and we still perform pagan rites associated with these occasions. Eggs and rabbits are symbols of fertility that exemplify the revival of nature in spring. Decoration of a non-deciduous tree is a symbol of survival through the winter.

Herodotus continues his description of the popular religion:

To these gods the Persians offer sacrifice in the following manner: they raise no altar, light no fire, pour no libations; there is no sound of the flute, no putting on of chaplets, no consecrated barley-cake; but the man who wishes to sacrifice brings his victim to a spot of ground which is pure from pollution, and there calls upon the name of the god to whom he intends to offer. It is usual to have the turban encircled with a wreath, most commonly of myrtle. The sacrificer is not allowed to pray for blessings on himself alone, but he prays for the welfare of the king, and of the whole Persian people, among whom he is of necessity included. He cuts the victim in pieces, and having boiled the flesh, he lays it out upon the tenderest herbage that he can find, trefoil especially. When all is ready, one of the Magi comes forward and chants a hymn, which they say recounts the origin of the gods. It is not lawful to offer sacrifice unless there is a Magus present. After waiting a short time the sacrificer carries the flesh of the victim away with him, and makes whatever use of it he may please.

To underline the point that Zoroastrianism coexisted with the old religion, Herodotus says:

There is another custom which is spoken of with reserve, and not openly, concerning their dead. It is said that the body of a male Persian is never buried, until it has been torn either by a dog or a bird of prey. That the Magi have this custom is beyond a doubt, for they practise it without any concealment. The dead bodies are covered with wax, and then buried in the ground.

The Magi are a very peculiar race, different entirely from the Egyptian priests, and indeed from all other men whatsoever. The Egyptian priests make it a point of religion not to kill any live animals except those which they offer in sacrifice. The Magi, on the contrary, kill animals of all kinds with their own hands, excepting dogs and men. They even seem to take a delight in the employment, and kill, as readily as they do other animals, ants and snakes, and such like flying or creeping things.

Clearly, the Magi called their own tune. However, not all Iranians followed these customs. When Alexander, having already traversed the whole of Iran, arrived to conquer Bactria, he encountered the towers of silence (where the dead were surrendered to scavenger animals) *for the first time,* expressing his revulsion and ordering an end to this practice.

God versus Satan

Being brought up with a typical polytheist pantheon, Zarathushtra was no stranger to the concept of a malevolent god. But he developed the idea further – his Angra Mainu (later Ahriman) is no mere vandal. He is no less than a commander of all that is evil, and his aim is nothing less than to undo the entire creation. Good men do not appease or worship him – they instead join God to oppose evil and all its works. It is nothing new now – but Zarathushtra's contemporaries heard it first.

Between the choices the seekers of false gods did not decide correctly because the lie came over their choosing. So they chose the bad mind, poured forth with wrath and afflicted the human existence. But to one who chooses rightly comes strength of body and ongoing calmness through strength, good mind and righteousness.

Of all these, such a person shall belong to God because he has passed the ordeal of fire.

(Gathas: iii)

More so, Zarathushtra appears to be the original author of a belief that the world should, sooner or later, end. He perceived this as an apocalyptic reckoning between good and evil, and it is a central tenet of his creed that good will finally triumph under the leadership of a Messiah, a heroic figure sent to spearhead the overthrow of Satan.

The cosmos of Sumerians and Egyptians had a well-defined beginning. But no one, ancient Hebrews included, considered the present world as a passing phase; it nearly comes to an end once, but after the great flood God promises that He will never lose His temper again. We can only take Him at His word.

Time was measured in seasons. Even the most sophisticated people of antiquity – Egyptians and Greeks – perceived time as a circular entity, rather than a linear scale. Years were numbered in lunar cycles or marked by coronation of a ruler, upon whose death the count was reset to zero. Even Romans used this system, referencing dates by the reigns of their consuls.

A continuous, linear calendar that runs from the beginning of time appears to be a Persian innovation, reputedly implemented at the time of the Seleucid rule. They used the date of Zarathushtra's birth as year zero, having obtained that date (mistakenly) as 539BC, from Babylonian archives. It was, in fact, the date when Cyrus conquered Babylon. This is the presumed origin of misconception about the chronology of Zoroastrianism.

Zarathushtra's other remarkable achievement lies in his emphasis on the worth and the autonomy of an individual. Although the Good God is the most powerful entity in the universe, it is not His nature or purpose to control or pre-determine the behaviour of other sentient beings, Satan included.

Because the Good God chooses not to control other beings, the struggle between good and evil is eternal and universal. That struggle will continue until the very end of the world as we know it. In this cosmic war there is no respite and no non-combatants. Each sentient being not only can – but must – make a choice.

In a possibly apocryphal conversation between a mainland Greek and a Persian, recorded somewhere in Asia Minor, the great interface between the two cultures, the Greek mocks the Persian for living under a despot, who holds the power of life or death over his subjects. The Greeks, he says, are free men (referring to Greece proper, rather than the Asia Minor colonies that were vassals of the Persian empire and generally ruled by approved tyrants).

The Persian replies that it may be so, but the free Greeks lead a meaningless life – not even their gods understand the purpose of their existence. But in Iran each righteous man, no matter how humble, is a soldier of God whose life serves an eternal purpose. Any such man can live his life with honour and with pride.

Wise God, whoever, man or woman, will give me what You know to be the best in life, rewards for righteousness, strength through good mind, I shall accompany him and her in glorifying You as You are, and will, with all of them, cross over the bridge of selection.

(Gathas: xi)

(The bridge of selection was crossed by the soul of the deceased, over a fiery chasm. One's deeds determined whether one fell in or made it to the other end.)

The beneficent man, who works for the realization of good mind and dominion, and serves righteousness with his words and actions. Such a man, Wise Lord, is the most useful person.

(Gathas: iv)

That is a remarkable affirmation of individual worth, especially for a creed of such early times. Not only is each human endowed with a dignity simply irrelevant to other faiths to this day, but Zoroastrianism neatly avoids the crucial discontinuity in the logic of Abrahamic religions, known as the Job Conundrum.

Put in simple terms, the Book of Job is a highly entertaining account (written late in the history of ancient Judaism – fifth, possibly fourth century BC) of a righteous man unjustly tested by God at Satan's behest. Alas, neither the Book of Job nor the rivers of ink spilled over this conundrum hence, make even the slightest progress in providing a rational explanation as to why bad things happen to good people, seemingly in inverse proportion to their goodness.

The best that Abrahamic theologians can do is suggest that ways of God are too complicated for the sorry likes of us, and the dilemma only appears to exist because we cannot see the wider picture.

Like the central tenet of Buddhism – that life incurs suffering – Zarathushtra's is also self-explanatory and self-evident: life is a struggle. God is not to blame for the appalling events in the world – He neither desires them nor takes pleasure in their occurrence.

They are not a part of any mysterious grand design – it's just that universal insurance is not God's nature or purpose. His followers are not sheep, but soldiers in an apocalyptic struggle. As their commander, He does not wish their demise at the hand of evil – it is simply unavoidable that some good men must fall in battle.

A Zoroastrian is not expected to "turn the other cheek" or stand in an orderly queue to a gas chamber. For a Zoroastrian there is no surprise or disappointment when he is confronted with appalling evil.

Being invited to become a cake of soap should not paralyse a follower of this creed – its prophet had warned that evil strides the earth, and nowhere does it say that it has boundaries:

Therefore, let none of you listen to the messages and teachings of the wrongful, because he brings danger and destruction to the house, settlement, region, and land. Correct him with weapons.

(Gathas: Song iv)

For a Zoroastrian an encounter with evil is a call to arms, not a trigger for a disabling crisis of faith at a time when survival hinges on instant action.

It follows from Zarathushtra's creed that vengeance is not left to God. On the contrary, it is a universal duty of men to right wrongs and to keep their environment clear of rogues and destroyers.

We have instant difficulty with this today. Since the beginning of the first millennium our world throve under the rule of Roman law and the successors to its legacy of an iron-fisted state. Whilst Romans were unencumbered with religious fervour, they fanatically obeyed and enforced their laws.

A Roman Emperor could have a law altered, but he could not openly disobey a law that was currently in force. A Roman citizen who broke the law did not merely take a short cut – he turned his back on an entire world and could expect severe and imminent punishment that he was, by modern standards, relatively unlikely to evade.

Such control made vigilantism redundant and foreign to our psyche, but we are now faced with a new reality that is far closer to Zarathushtra's in structure.

The power of a large state has been undermined by technology. As that technology becomes cheaper and mass-produced, weapons that made modern empires supreme are trickling into the hands of the world's poorest and most backward people, whose anger at the glittering lights of an industrial civilization has turned them into vicious predators. The use of technology by modern criminals and modern terrorists has shifted the onus in prevention of crime onto responsible citizens.

The state cannot adapt or react with sufficient speed, and the overall reaction to these developments appears to fall back on classic Indo-European tools of military conquest and cultural conversion. It is possible that a hypervigilant state may have made 9/11 more difficult and less costly – after all, acts of terrorism were rare in USSR and Nazi Germany.

It is unwise for Muslim fanatics to pin Islam to their bombs. That presents the West with a logical response to their threat – define the Islamic world as a target and bomb it into oblivion. Likewise, Muslim minorities in

Western countries are easy and relatively helpless targets in the face of an angry state.

It is possible to win a war against foreign terrorism through reciprocal terror. Nazi troops occupying Eastern Europe had effectively stemmed guerilla actions by massacring large numbers of civilians in response to each attack on German troops. It is conceivably possible to practise retribution with such intensity that any sectarian terrorist would be deterred by the likely consequences for his native community.

But it is harder to deal with terror perpetrated by angry men of no particular colour or creed. It is not possible for any state that still calls itself free to prevent Timothy McVeighs – that can only be done, to the extent that it can be at all, by a society with a high ethical standard and a high level of social responsibility.

History will pass harsh judgement on the modern anti-terrorist industry. All over the Western world the state is becoming more intrusive and more oblivious of human rights than the terrorists who supposedly threaten it. Inevitably, the attitudes of the controllers slide into abuse of the controlled.

Arguably, the result is worse than terrorism, being the worst threat to pluralism for three hundred years. It is unclear how the rise of the rabid state can be stemmed, with Western societies rapidly sliding back towards the ancient

Indo-European identity – a terrifying sight in the age of ballistic missiles commanded by barely literate men.

Surviving Zoroastrian literature

During conquest of Persia its royal libraries were destroyed by Alexander's troops. Unfortunately, that included most of the sacred texts, only fragments of which are available today. Some of the surviving texts (probably preserved in verbal form) are in Avestan, an Iranian language of such antiquity that some passages cannot be translated to this day. Avestan resembles Sanskrit of early second millennium BC, suggesting the authenticity of such texts, possibly all the way back to Zarathushtra's lifetime. They are believed to have been transmitted orally for centuries before they found written form, possibly even without being fully understood.

Not surprisingly, the surviving sacred library is somewhat disjointed. Some attribute the lack of success of Zoroastrianism in attracting followers to this confusion – a rational individual shopping for a religion may view its library with great consternation. But destruction has afflicted other religions too – what the Zoroastrians are *not* guilty of is editing and censoring the surviving materials to present a marketable version. Their refusal to do so shows real commitment to the moral precepts of their religion, in contrast to Christian clerics who redrafted their creed to suit the politics of the day – and ruthlessly destroyed precious historical materials that conflicted with their immediate needs.

The first attempt to reconstitute holy Zoroastrian texts destroyed by Alexander was made some centuries later. A few revisions on, the holy texts as we know them today were assembled by the third century AD. They are not at all complete, and they too had to be rescued from the next calamity to befall Iran – the Arab invasion.

The surviving library of Iranian sacred texts is called The Avesta, similar to the Hebrew Bible in that it is not one book but many.

Most of the ancient sacred texts destroyed during Alexander's invasion were reconstituted in the reign of Vologeses I (51-80 AD). The content of Avesta was then finalized in the reign of great Sassanid king Shapur II (309-379 AD). The modern Avesta is considered a relatively small remnant of the Shapur compilation, most of its contents believed to be lost during the Arab invasion.

The Avesta is generally divided into five groups:

1. Yasna, the main compilation with 72 chapters. Fourteen Yasnas are called the Gathas, ancient hymns believed to be composed by Zarathushtra in person.

2. Visparad, a collection of commentaries on the

Yasna.

3. The Yashts, hymns that praise Zoroastrian immortals (equivalent to angels of Christianity).

4. The Vendidad, a book listing evil spirits and the means of protection against them.

5. "Miscellaneous" prayers, texts, prayers, and benedictions.

The Arabs had an even more pressing reason to erase the Zoroastrian legacy. Mohammed heavily borrowed from Zoroastrianism, directly as well as through Judaic and Christian sources. He well realized the danger Zoroastrianism presented to his project.

Mohammed barely concealed his contempt for faiths of the other "People of the Book" – Jews and Christians. His commentary on Jesus leaves no doubt on this score, and his thoughts about Jews are not, fortunately, given wide currency in the Moslem world.

But Zoroastrians, who are not mentioned in the Koran at all, were a different matter. Here Mohammed saw a genuine rival for the hearts and minds of his desert warriors. That may be the reason why the Christian regions won by Moslem armies were preserved almost intact, an Arab emir taking over from the Greek governor with nothing destroyed or defaced – yet a bloodbath and systematic destruction of cultural artefacts took place when Arabs conquered Iran a short time later.

In his classic work on Persian history, J.M. Cook calls the ancient Persians unintellectual, attempting to account for the lack of authentic record or enduring works of original literary art.

This is a splendid example of European arrogance. There are, as mentioned, few surviving artefacts that shed light on the everyday life in Carthage, only one Carthaginian document surviving in fragmented translation. Yet we know that Carthaginians, the inventors of the alphabet, had extensive libraries.

Like many other cultural attributes, literacy spread into Iran came from Mesopotamia – where writing was not a universal skill because learning the prevalent script was no small investment of effort (made deliberately so by those who made a living out of writing). Unlike Semites and Greeks, the Persians originally wrote in cuneiform borrowed from Babylonians, a semi-hieroglyphic script not widely taught in their population – a tradition only partially changed by the adaptation of the Phoenician alphabet to Aramaic later.

The real crime of Persian literati was the early adoption of ox hide, in preference to more durable materials such as clay tablets. Hides burned in their thousands when Alexander rampaged through Persia. By contrast, a gigantic library of clay tablets survived the destruction of Nineveh, the capital of Assyria – whose culture no one accuses of excessive sophistication.

The general fragility of ancient sources is hard to conceive today, when each newspaper lining an old suitcase contains enough material for a PhD of some future archaeologist.

It is a miracle that men of the calibre of Cyrus or Ramses II left more than semi-legendary memories – the graves of both survived to be explored by modern science. Ramses even had the ignominy of being autopsied and X-Rayed.

Every now and again it is possible to unearth an archive such as the palace library at Nineveh. Its giant stack of clay tablets was contemptuously ignored by their conquerors, not unlike the treasure trove of multilingual records from Amarna in Egypt.

The clay and stone archives of the Hittites were likewise ignored by the Phrygians who overran their capital. Decipherment, based on what the Hittite language has in common with modern German, opened a remarkable window into the daily life of this early Indo-European culture, much as an archive of a regional newspaper would showcase our world for a future discoverer, once he managed to understand the purpose of the sports section.

It is most fortuitous that today we have a chiselled copy of the laws of Hammurabi and a foundation block of a building ceremonially laid and inscribed by Pontius Pilate. Even though such artefacts were made in large numbers in their day – a stone block with the laws of Hammurabi would have graced every population centre of his kingdom, and even a procurator as unpopular as Pilate would have laid many foundation stones in his capacity as Caesar's representative in Judea. The famous trilingual Rosetta stone was found by pure accident. It was recycled by being incorporated into a foundation wall, which got in the way of Napoleon's soldiers building fortifications two thousand years later.

Archaeological artefacts that confirm events described in the Hebrew Bible are remarkably few in number, despite monumental efforts to find them. There is one single building block from a ruined fortress with an inscription referring to a descendant of King David. That stone is one of a handful artefacts that testify to the existence of the entire dynasty of David.

Another such treasure is the stone of Moab that mentions the Israelites contemporary to Mesha, the king of the Moabites from eighth century BC. Assyrian archives also make mention of Israelites, who spearheaded an anti-Assyrian coalition at the battle of Karkar.

The Hebrew Bible had only been written down between sixth and fourth centuries BC. The oldest authentic version of it is the copper Dead Sea scroll of the Book of Isaiah, which is dated to around 100 BC. The oldest complete version of the Hebrew Bible dates from eleventh century AD – sixteen centuries after the initial written compilation and possibly twenty-five centuries after the original oral traditions began to appear.

With that background, it is easy to appreciate the apparent continuity of the Gathas. Persians were largely preliterate until the time of Cyrus. It is a miracle that we possess anything of ancient Zoroastrian texts, written down at the edict of Cyrus, somewhere around 550 BC.

Despite being destroyed and reconstructed only two centuries later, probably from fragments and oral form, they leave Zoroastrianism much better documented than Judaism. We do not have any authentic texts by Moses, for instance – they were rewritten in contemporary Hebrew as late as fifth century BC. If Moses did pen any texts, they do not survive in the original form, unlike the Avestan Gathas.

Now, oral tradition of ancient people seems reliable enough – no more and no less reliable than modern scholarship. In modern times we may have the technology for flawless reproduction of materials, but we also have biases that can cause a profound loss of transmitted information.

In preliterate cultures a sacred text or a record of some earth-shaking event is memorized by many individuals simultaneously, and distortion of that information can only occur in an incremental manner, through linguistic shift, slight embellishment or omission when the text is handed down. It is not possible to simply revise the text to suit one's purpose – that would be seen as a sacrilege by one's contemporaries equally familiar with the story.

The Stone of Moab (@ 850BC). Its text records the victory by King Mesha in a border skirmish with the neighbouring Israelites.

The Cyrus Cylinder (539BC), described as containing the first charter of human rights.

Zarathushtra – an Indo-European

At first glance, Zoroastrianism is a strange creed to emerge where and when it did, given the violent and chaotic context of contemporary Iranian society.

Iranians belong to a very large family of cultures known as Indo-Europeans, a linguistic group discovered and named in the eighteenth century by a British judge who studied Sanskrit (the ancient and sacred language of India, from which most Indian languages are derived), between his duties on the bench in colonial India. These duties could not have been as onerous as they are today, for the judge soon noticed many similarities between Sanskrit and ancient Greek along with Latin, both of which he knew well from his schooling.

The massive movement that spread these languages began some time in the third millennium BC. Indo-Europeans experienced something of a stasis by the time of Zarathushtra – much as they do today.

Contrary to Nazi ravings, Indo-Europeans do not constitute a race – they are, instead, a diverse group of nations who speak related languages. As we will explore, there are other common characteristics to Indo-European culture, but languages remain the main way to identify populations in that ethnic grouping.

Experts in this field try not to acknowledge what anyone with an ounce of common sense is forced to conclude – Indo-Europeans are more than speakers of related languages. They appear to share certain cultural traits, and these traits have persevered through four millennia of Indo-European peregrinations.

Many Indo-European nations such as Russia are, in fact, multiracial quilts, made up of subcultures that represent every colour and creed – yet their basic behaviour remains true to the Indo-European form of their umbrella culture.

Few people would consider the late Rudolf Nureev anything but a leading light of European culture. Yet he called himself a Tatar – a mainly Muslim ethnic group claiming its ancestry from Mongols who once ruled Russia. Likewise, many of today's Britons are blends of at least two races – yet they play cricket and eat fish with chips. Their descendants will consider themselves just as British as the people whose genetic profile links them to Neolithic remains found in the caves in the English countryside.

Minorities absorbed into Indo-European cultures take on the fundamental Indo-European characteristics. As we will see shortly, crucial aspects of their collective behaviour become thoroughly and stereotypically Indo-European.

Sometimes that fact is obscured by religious, racial or geographic factors. A bigot will have great difficulty accepting that Pakistani tribesmen are no more "Asiatic" than Russians or even Germans, or that Indians are truer "Aryans" than some Scandinavians. Yet this is so.

Today the world is increasingly classified as Western or Islamic. This is not new – the battle between Islam and the West began shortly after the birth of Islam, and it had only briefly abated in the nineteenth century, when Turkey, the flag bearer of Islam, found itself outgunned by Western powers. Other Islamic nations were either not at all able to oppose European powers or were occupied by them as colonies.

That short, fifty-year break in the war between the West and Islam abruptly ended after World War II. Its resumption is traditionally blamed on the founding of Israel, a country that may be regarded as a colony of Russian Jews in formerly Muslim territory.

A more objective analysis suggests that the departure of colonial powers from Islamic countries left the latter free to pursue their old agenda, now bolstered with petrodollars. The conflict has since escalated to levels comparable to past intensity, with exchanges of fire between Western and Islamic armies becoming too mundane to make the news. Muslims who emigrated to the West are increasingly regarded as unwanted aliens, with traditionally orderly societies like Germany and Australia experiencing street violence motivated by a religious divide.

One of the complexities in this struggle is that classifying people on the basis of Islam does not seem to be very predictive of their national psychology, even though such ignorance led to predictable consequences every time.

Despite professing Islam for centuries, most Muslims of Eurasia remain firmly Indo-European. One need not wonder why Afghans and Chechens proved so adept in warfare against Indo-Europeans, or why the Turks are so incensed by their exclusion from European Union.

The reason is simple: these are still Indo-European people, whose behaviour is not fully explained by Islam any more than another Semitic religion, Christianity, explains the behaviour of their European opponents.

The Aryan myth constructed in Germany is another false divide, for many of the nations consigned by Nazi ideologues to the status of inferior beings are fellow Indo-Europeans: Slavs, Gypsies (who originated in India), and even Jews themselves.

The latter assertion deserves further exploration. Whilst the original inhabitants of ancient Israel and Judea spoke Semitic languages (first Hebrew, then Aramaic as lingua franca), for at least 2,500 years their social milieu was thoroughly Indo-European – Iranian, Greek, Roman, Slavic and Germanic.

By the end of the nineteenth century nearly all European Jews spoke an Indo-European language, Yiddish (which, despite containing loan words from Hebrew, is officially listed as a dialect of German, easily comprehensible to any speaker of that language).

It is not in dispute that of the estimated seventy million Jews living today, those speaking Hebrew as a native language comprise just three million, the rest having spoken their first words in Spanish, French, German, English or Russian.

Language aside, Israel is a European society in lifestyle and outlook, with institutions firmly rooted in a liberal Western foundation. Indeed, it has recently applied to be a member of the European Union, despite, technically, being located in Africa. Likewise, it has applied to join the British Commonwealth, despite only being occupied by the British for a short 30 years.

Arabs are entirely correct when they insist that Israel is more of an affront to their world than Outremer, the Crusader state that occupied similar borders a millennium before. The latter, after all, was just a bandit enclave run by armoured thugs, little different from the surrounding enclaves run by Muslim warlords from whom Outremer heavily borrowed. The Crusaders came to the Middle East entirely unencumbered by culture, and cultural exchange with their Muslim neighbours went more or less one way.

Israelis, on the other hand, came from modern Europe to an Arab world stuck in early Middle Ages. They set up a noisy, pluralistic democracy with a generous welfare state that delivers excellent results in literacy, health care and due process – three foundations of any successful society today. These successes stand in an embarrassing contrast to Israel's neighbours, who live much as they did at the time of the Crusades.

Furthermore, Israel appears to enjoy an overwhelming military advantage over the entire region, something the Crusaders could not even imagine. Their survival depended solely on the lack of unity amongst their Muslim neighbours. Israel, on the contrary, had faced a united attack by all of its neighbours not once but three times – and defeated them utterly.

It is no surprise that its presence is feared and resented more than that of Crusaders. Arabs have no illusions about Israelis being a fellow Semitic people. They recognize Israel as an outpost of a global culture that one crosses only after finalizing one's affairs.

Indo-Europeans are not merely speakers of related languages, but a highly distinctive cultural grouping. Its behaviour, especially military, appears to distinguish it from other cultural groups.

What constitutes the winning formula behind Indo-European success requires a study of history and sociology to a standard of objectivity and integrity not available today. Sadly, many leading scholars of relevant disciplines consider themselves above basic rules of academic conduct. Their crude bias heavily interferes with our understanding of fundamental trends that shaped our origins.

Nowhere is this more damaging than in our inability to accept the Indo-European phenomenon in all its horror and all its glory. Unless we accept these truths, we are unable to consider how Indo-European culture may evolve, in order to achieve glory without the accompanying horror.

However, it does not require genius to conclude that the unusual (if not unique) cultural traits, especially those related to pursuit of war, are the likely drivers behind the global expansion of Indo-European culture.

It is time to go where scholars don't dare to tread,

beginning with a list of characteristics common to Indo-Europeans, ancient and modern.

Indo-European expansion – the motives

The reason why three quarters of the world population learn an Indo-European language from birth is not the convenience of Indo-European linguistic form – which, in fact, is relatively unwieldy.

The reason, instead, is that Indo-Europeans usually won. After conquest they forced the conquered nation to adopt crucial elements of their culture. These adoptions were cemented in place by success (in evolutionary terms) of Indo-European social structures and, more often than not, a higher standard of living that resulted.

Throughout the span of written history, the military odds came down heavily against non-Indo-Europeans. The exceptions merely prove the rule – Semitic Carthaginians, so thoroughly destroyed that their culture has to be reconstructed from shards, Mongols, whose descendants are now a tiny nation in the shadow of Russia they once ruled, and Japanese, now more Western than the West.

Arabs? That chapter is not yet complete. But after thirteen centuries of conflict, few observers would predict an Arabic-speaking planet in the future. All indicators suggest that instead, the ultimate destiny of Arab culture resembles that of its cousin, Carthage.

The key to understanding the Indo-European expansion is deceptively simple: Indo-European invaders were always a tiny minority in a vast territory.

They descended on their victims with great speed, achieved overwhelming victories within a short time frame and so subsumed the native cultures that today we can merely guess what some of those looked like.

In most cases the newcomers left virtually no genetic legacy. Now, this is difficult to imagine for us, brought up on stories of native genocide by European settlers in recent times.

In the past four centuries migrants from an industrial Europe invaded sparsely populated landscapes inhabited by Stone Age tribes. These natives were subjugated by professional armies equipped with horses, metal armour, firearms, and centuries of accumulated expertise of fighting organized wars. After the guns fell silent, the natives were decimated by diseases from across the world that were new to their gene pool. Survivors had to cope with a totally alien culture, one that overwhelmed the coping mechanisms honed in a relatively static tribal milieu.

Overt resistance was futile, and the best that such native people could do was preserve knowledge of their customs in a token manner, whilst being otherwise absorbed into the invading society – with relative success, as in North America and New Zealand, or as dismal failure, as in Australia or South Africa.

Finally, modern invaders were not particularly interested in the natives' fate – at best the latter were regarded as a source of unreliable labour, and at worst as pests that impeded an orderly exploitation of conquered territory. Their cultural heritage was considered worthless, to be preserved – at best – out of scientific curiosity.

One needs to draw a clear distinction between modern and ancient conquerors: few ancient invasions resulted in a wholesale replacement of the native population. Unlike the en-masse export of surplus Europeans to colonies in modern era, ancient invaders arrived in much smaller numbers, and few of them could make entire nations vanish even when desired – which they seldom did.

In ancient times an army seldom numbered more than a few tens of thousands. To begin with, ancient populations were many orders of magnitude smaller than today. Then it was a simple matter of logistics: ancient societies were very different in their ability to generate surplus resources, marshal and transport armies or even maintain the health of soldiers bundled together in unsanitary conditions.

There are ancient reports of armies containing a million men, such as the reputed army of Xerxes, the successful invader of Greece, or 500,000 soldiers lined up in the battle of Châlons, where Attila was turned back from his demolition of Roman Europe. Such figures are not credible.

The supply lines during the last world war sustained such numbers in the field for the first time – but this was only possible because of the internal combustion engine, the rail and the telephone, not to mention modern agriculture and four of the world's largest economies – and even then they frequently failed at crucial times, such as during the Battle of the Bulge. It was estimated that during that campaign the Allies burned 20 litres of fuel for every litre delivered to the front.

To win a battle one army needs to defeat another. But to win a war, it needs to defeat the enemy to such an extent that no further resistance is feasible, at least on a large scale.

Today that means capturing or killing enemy personnel, equipment, strategic locations and assets – a modern victory is a combination of all of the above. There are many modern examples that show how little a partial victory is worth. One can certainly overwhelm the defences of a nation like Iraq and occupy its entire territory. Alas, that did not mean the end of the war in Iraq.

In ancient times massed forces met on a battlefield, the objective being to damage the opposing army to the point of it being unable to function as a unit, either through loss of low-ranking personnel or even the commander (who often lead the army into battle).

Ancient combatants also practised denial of access to basic resources, such as water or population centres containing supplies. As Rome proved with Hannibal, victory could be a matter of denying an ancient invader resources, particularly food, long enough to damage his ability to keep men in the ranks.

But most battles of antiquity resulted in relatively limited loss of life. At some point it became clear to one side that their cause is lost, and they would simply flee the battlefield. Gathering them back into a functional unit was seldom feasible in time or at all, especially if troops did not wish to regroup.

In ancient times escaping soldiers were not usually pursued. The main object was to break up the opponent's fighting unit and thus unseat the leader. Military prisoners, especially battle-hardened soldiers, made dangerous slaves. Their control was difficult before the age of rapid-fire weapons, and they could only be dispersed amongst less martial slaves. Alternatively, they were used up in specific situations such as desert mines or galleys of ships, where they had little opportunity to rebel and escape.

Massacres were not the objective, although they happened often enough when escape en-masse was impeded by terrain. Practically-minded invaders were reluctant to risk further losses through pursuit of desperate men, who were fleeing the field of battle.

More likely than not, the fleeing soldiers were local farmers and craftsmen, and without them the conquered land lost much of its value. The conquerors of antiquity wanted the wealth of the land as much as the land per se. Invaders did not, as a rule, have a surplus population to replace those they killed in conquest. Massacres, mass enslavement and mass exile were specific punishments for resistance, and they were perpetrated at invader's expense. Genocide of indigenous populations with economic motivation is a modern practice by those whose technology allows exploitation of land without aboriginal cooperation.

There are famous exceptions, which distort our perception. Hannibal's expedition into Italy was marked by severe (and probably accurately documented) losses on the Roman side, and this reflects the passions on both sides of that war – Hannibal's fierce hatred of Rome and an equally fierce resistance of a nation that never compromised, as a definition of its national psyche.

Assyrians are another exception. As a terror tactic they massacred armies and populations of those who resisted. The purpose was to terrify other enemies, already conquered and otherwise, into submission, for Assyrians themselves were never a large nation. The monstrous reputation they carefully cultivated was an important plank in their strategy, which allowed them to achieve regional dominance. They were superb fighters – but by no means irresistible or invincible, their empire suffering numerous twists and turns of military fortune until eventually subsumed by former vassals.

After battle – ancient armies seldom fought after dark – the victors regrouped and settled into a protected camp to rest. They did not chase the scattered enemy, especially those who disarmed and fled at full speed from men bearing heavy armour and weapons. The next day the victorious army would take possession of spoils, usually by occupying whatever remained of the vanquished army's camp, then they would march through the territory they now owned.

It was possible to rally survivors to fight again, but this always took time and effort. The enemy now commanded resources such as fortified points, water sources and food supplies. A vanquished leader was likely to be discredited by his loss, and men would need to be persuaded to return to his banner. There were no practical means to compel them – hunting down deserters is something that requires modern information systems and modern police methods. In ancient times authorities had few means of verifying identity, changing which was a matter of moving a distance from one's home. If the defeated party lost control over its territory, desertion went unpunished altogether.

Therefore, breaking an army in the field was usually sufficient to secure victory. The invader would then establish regional control of conquered territory through deployment of relatively small units in strategic locations.

Ancient empire builders were not always motivated by population pressures at home. Italy, for instance, suffered from a low population density during the period of maximal territorial expansion of the Roman Empire. Alexander's motives were not in the slightest about exporting surplus Macedonians or Greeks.

In ancient times invasion of a far-away land was seldom a practical way to export a surplus population. Such exports were achieved by frustrating means – by foot and wagon, as was the case in the Goth migrations, or by ship, as was the case with Phoenician and Greek colonies throughout the Mediterranean Basin. Ancient ships could not carry more than a few dozen passengers – a far cry from British flotillas that could carry ten times that number of immigrants to distant lands as easily as they could carry them across the English Channel.

In summary, ancient invaders came in much smaller numbers than we envisage today. Ancient populations remained genetically static, only changing their cultures – either when forced to do so or when given sufficient incentive, such as superior standard of living enjoyed by the conqueror.

This is an important point, as one of the main barriers to understanding the Indo-European culture lies in the apparent diversity of modern Indo-Europeans. Yet a chocolate-hued Singhalese shares certain crucial characteristics with a Dane – which the Dane does not share with his neighbouring non-Indo-European Finn.

Indo-European expansion – the mechanics

The "weighed mean" of expert opinion places the original Indo-Europeans, known as Proto-Indo-Europeans, somewhere at the foot of mineral-rich Ural Range, in a steppe (flat grassland) bordering heavily forested mountains.

The weighed mean goes on to suggest that some time around 2500 BC Proto-Indo-Europeans spawned great waves of successive migration – one westwards, into Europe, the other to the south – into Central Asia, Iranian plateau and India.

We know virtually nothing else about Proto-Indo-Europeans as living people. We have graves of extinct cultures with simple goods. From the character of these it is deduced that these cultures represent early Indo-Europeans, but their exact position in the Indo-European family tree is unknown. There is certainly nothing about these grave goods that would explain the subsequent success of Indo-Europeans.

Proto-Indo-Europeans were probably semi-nomads, most likely Caucasians. It is easier to state what they were – a people who excelled in violence and revelled in it with utter contempt for human life. Whenever they occupied new territory, the population soon changed its culture to that of the invaders, creating a vast ocean of nations with common characteristics of their collective psychology, stretching from Britain and Norway to the southern tip of the Indian subcontinent.

Their greatest triumph, which populated much of Eurasia with speakers of Indo-European languages, preceded the development of writing by at least one millennium. The earliest documentation of oral Indo-European began around 1700 BC with the Indian Rig Veda, followed by the Hittites, whose royal archives date to around 1500 BC, then the early Greek literature from around 800 BC. These dates are based mainly on linguistic analysis of surviving texts. There are no surviving documents from the early Vedic age. Likewise, Homer is known from texts written many centuries after his death.

Mittani kingdom, which lay north-west of Mesopotamia, was a nation of probably Semitic people, ruled by an Indo-European elite. It is from there that we appear to have the earliest original documents (clay tablets in cuneiform script used in Mesopotamia) that refer to Indo-European gods and clearly Indo-European names.

 A thousand years of early Indo-European history is missing from written record, and this imposes profound limitations on what we will ever know about its prehistoric ancestors, the Proto-Indo-

Europeans. The archaeological record is not entirely unhelpful, but it is limited by tiny population sizes, sparse use of durable materials, and the nomadic nature of Proto-Indo-Europeans.

Nevertheless, it is impossible to escape the conclusion that they were accomplished practitioners of violence. Much as experts on the Indo-European phenomenon try to distract themselves from this fact, no amount of political correctness can massage away reality: the business of Proto-Indo-Europeans and their descendants – modern-day ones very much included – is conquest and cultural subjugation.

Indo-Europeans went into the business of building multi-cultural empires at a much later time. For the first two millennia they were in the business of erasing indigenous cultures and replacing them with their own.

Despite fierce challenges from Semitic speakers (Carthaginians and Arabs) and speakers of Altaic languages (Mongolian and Turkic), today's world is, unabashedly, an Indo-European village, whose technology and collective behaviour are heavily Indo-European.

It is a fact that only small pockets of non-Indo-European cultures remain on the entire face of Europe. Only three European nations officially speak a non-Indo-European tongue: Hungary, Finland and Estonia. The latter two are believed to be survivors of the Indo-European invasion, their Ugro-Finnic culture withstanding the conquerors. Hungarians, on the other hand, arrived after Indo-Europeans and retained a pocket of non-Indo-European speakers in Europe.

There are two minorities of political significance in Europe. The Basques are believed to be another remnant of pre-Indo-European population, possibly the aborigines of Europe. They were forced, probably from a much larger territory, into the mountains, where advantages of military techniques favoured by Indo-Europeans were negated by the terrain. Likewise the Saami people of Finland and Norway are Uralic language speakers, relatives of other aborigines of northern Eurasia, who still live in abundance in Russian Siberia. They were forced out from more hospitable lands into sub-Arctic territory, which the invaders evidently judged unworthy of continued effort.

Out of the most influential modern nations, only Japan and China can be classified as non-Indo-European, although the amount of borrowing from Indo-Europeans into these cultures makes the statement almost meaningless.

The world balance of power is, without doubt, in Indo-European hands, and it has rested there for over two hundred years. Recent population growth in the non-Indo-European world has failed to alter that power balance.

It is thus evident that the Indo-European phenomenon is the most significant component of human history during the past five thousand years, both in terms of size and significance. Yet collated understanding of it is very recent – the ink is barely dry on first accessible works on this subject.

The main reason for this is abuse of history at the hands of two totalitarian regimes. Nazis usurped the Aryan name (Arii being the Proto-Indo-European cognomen for its people, the word "Iran" still being a derivation of this root). Nazi pseudo-science was built up from a collection of racist musings of assorted would-be anthropologists of the nineteenth century, glued together with the Übermensch (Superman) ravings of Nietzsche, who wrote his salient works whilst he was suffering from cerebral syphilis.

Nietzsche's signature work, "Thus Spoke Zarathustra" turned a champion of equality and universal decency into intellectual fig leaf of National Socialism. Nietzsche may have read Zoroastrian texts, translated into European languages some forty years before. If so, his choice of Zarathushtra as a mouthpiece is bizarre – to say the least.

Nietzsche's own explanation was that

Zarathustra was the man who hailed the birth of morality, and he should return, metaphorically, to announce its death. I am not sure I can follow that logic, and it is much more parsimonious to conclude that cerebral syphilis was a ghost writer who stood behind the famous German philosopher. I leave it to the interested reader to determine where Nietzsche's philosophy ends and where insanity begins.

Suffice it to say that there is no connection whatsoever with the tenets of Zoroastrianism and Nietzsche's belief – that the moral age was an evolutionary dead end, and the way forward lies through the triumph of super humans who are not constrained by principle. All this is especially offensive to a Zoroastrian mindset.

There are two reasons to take these writings with a large grain of salt. Apart from evidence of extensive post-mortem redaction by Nietzsche's sister, an anti-Semitic ideologue, all of his output should be examined with a view to the effects of cerebral syphilis.

It is a slow disease that does not usually result in explosive psychotic episodes. Rather, there is a gradual evolution of bizarre (or unconventional) behaviour, one classic manifestation being "folie de grandeur", the delusion of grandeur.

Syphilis was endemic prior to introduction of penicillin. Society was essentially divided into known syphilitics, potential syphilitics (such as promiscuous people) and unlikely syphilitics (such as virgins from "good" families, the disease usually being passed from mother to foetus). Intercourse with a syphilitic is highly likely to result in transmission, although syphilis can also be spread by poor hygiene or through professional contact, resulting in delicious ambiguities, such as "where did the doc get his chancre"?

Only the end-stage syphilitics spent their days drooling in dark corners of mental asylums. What precedes such a state, by many years or even decades, is a much more subtle behavioural disorder. It is quite different to the collapse of a functioning personality one frequently sees with dementia or schizophrenia.

People with cerebral syphilis wrote, composed, made speeches in parliaments and commanded armies, often with little apparent loss of skill or creativity. Witness Schubert's Unfinished Symphony, written shortly before his death from cerebral syphilis.

Nietzsche's works make far more sense when read with insight into this disease, his captivating style of prose notwithstanding. The choice of Zarathustra as a mouthpiece for amorality remains bizarre, even if understood as a deliberate insult to traditional morality. A more likely explanation is that he chose the more obscure Zarathustra because he was a soft target. Most of the contemporary audience would not have understood the incongruity.

The Nazi ideas about Aryan perfection fall more than a little flat when one considers that the historical Aryans may have been Asiatic. Wherever Proto-Indo-Europeans came from, Northern Europe represented a final stop in the western arm of their conquest.

Unfortunately, the bombastic image of blood and iron, rampaging warriors, a race born to conquer and rule, contains a core of historical truth. That is, after all, what transpired – but because of Nazi propaganda it became unfashionable to talk about Aryans, especially their military prowess. That taboo was especially strong in the Soviet Union, where the Nazi orgy left indelible scars on the national psyche – and where most remains of Proto-Indo-European cultures are located.

In fact, Soviet archaeologists had performed an immense amount of labour by digging up, studying and describing early Indo-European cultures, but none of these materials were readily available outside USSR until its collapse, being mostly published only in Russian. Whilst such work was not interfered with per se, historians were not permitted to synthesize disparate findings into a concept of Indo-European identity until the Soviet Union collapsed. The past decade saw a tremendous efflux of material from

Russian sources.

It is not possible to discuss this body of work without mentioning Arkaim, the site of earliest known Indo-European settlement yet discovered in Europe. The modern town of Arkaim lies close to the Russian border with Kazakhstan, at the foot of the Urals. This location matches both legendary sources and ethnographic tracking of Proto-Indo-European origin – all lines pointing to the origin of Indo-Europeans intersect in a region, whose centre is one thousand kilometres west of Arkaim (bearing in mind that the Indo-European migration began at least 500 years before it was built).

Arkaim's habitation is dated 1900 to 1700BC, some eight centuries after the great Indo-European migrations. It was burned and abandoned (indicating a sticky end for its inhabitants). There are other, smaller, such remains in the same locale. This may be the closest snapshot, in time and place, of Proto-Indo-European heartland.

Up to a thousand people may have dwelt in it, a relatively high population density for the ambient terrain. Arkaim's ruins are those of a well-defended fort, arranged around a single spiral street that winds 720 degrees, the outer diameter being approximately 200 meters. Its four-metre high walls of rammed earth packed into timber framing speak of a considerable preoccupation with defence, as does its cleverly designed curved entrance. An attacker who penetrates the outer defences must execute a sharp turn to the left. A horseman charging the entrance would have to come to a near-complete stop, therefore presenting an attractive stationary target to the cross-fire from the walls.

The most interesting feature of Arkaim houses is a revolutionary kiln structure found in most dwellings, consistent with reputation of Indo-Europeans as metal workers. An air tunnel between the furnace and the smelting well maximizes the temperature attained from burning fuel, presumably wood, with slag heaps and other artefacts of an established metal industry abundant nearby.

The burials nearby make it clear that Arkaim's inhabitants were consummate horsemen, and the ruins of the neighbouring settlement of Sintashta yielded what is probably the oldest military chariot ever found.

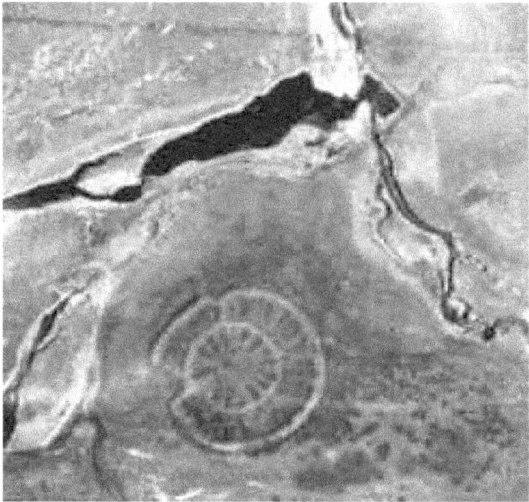

An aerial photograph of Arkaim prior to excavations. Note the spiral street pattern and the location between two nearby rivers.

Above: Aryan symbols found in Arkaim. Below: a model of a chariot found at Sintashta. It is believed to be the earliest war chariot ever found.

Above: Remains of a metalworker's kiln found in Arkaim and a selection of statues found in the vicinity. Below: shamanistic statuettes, Arkaim site.

Technological characteristics of early Indo-European societies

All documented Indo-European cultures display certain characteristics that may be linked to their success. They constitute technical innovations and social characteristics which may be identified amongst Indo-Europeans to this day:

I.   Domestication of the horse and specific use of horse for military purposes.

Indo-Europeans "rode" this advantage until outdone by latter nomads – Arabs, Mongols and Turks.

II.   Furthermore, they invented the spoked wheel, used in light horse-drawn war chariots, as opposed to means of transportation.

The invention of the chariot moved warfare into a new phase. As opposed to the mounted rider, the charioteer can travel at greater speed and wield projectile weapons with far greater accuracy (for the same amount of training). Chariots are also an effective weapon of intimidation, as well as being less vulnerable, in some ways, to counter-tactics.

Chariots are believed to have been first implemented around 2,000 BC, in the steppe region of modern Southern Russia and Ukraine, a terrain ideally suited to chariot warfare. It is a vast expanse of grassland with firm soil and little rock. The same region hosted the greatest tank battles in history four thousand years later. One can ponder how little the world had changed.

Mesopotamian chariots are much older, but these are ungainly and heavy constructions with wheels of solid wood. They are drawn by entirely unprotected (and slow) onagers, rather than horses. They appear to be a personnel carrier, if not a truck – not at all an offensive weapon.

The steppe dwellers appear to have done far more for the wheel's reputation. Even in Chinese, words that refer to this technology are borrowed from Indo-Europeans. The Proto-Indo-European root for circular motion was "rota", and we use it five thousand years on, to describe the motion – rotation.

III. Indo-Europeans appear to have kept themselves abreast of the latest in metallurgy, leading to earlier use of bronze and iron, compared with the cultures Indo-Europeans faced in their expansion.

As a general statement, many early Indo-Europeans enjoyed significant military advantage because of their metallurgical techniques. There is a record of correspondence between the Egyptian Pharaoh and a Hittite king, in which the former asks if any iron swords can be sent his way, and the Hittite replies that there was something of a poor season as far as iron is concerned. It was clearly highly prized.

The reason for iron displacing bronze is not as simple as the textbooks portray. Iron ore is more abundant and more ubiquitous in the world than tin, an essential component of hard bronze. Iron requires higher temperatures to smelt, and this is not the end of the story – iron has to be tempered into steel to offer an advantage over bronze. Once the technique of steel-making was mastered, there was a guaranteed local supply of military-grade metal.

Prior to the Iron Age, ancient people went a long way to get metals for bronze manufacture. For instance, Phoenicians went as far as Cornwall for tin. The main source of copper in the Mediterranean Basin was Cyprus. It ceased to export copper some time around the twelfth century BC – which coincides neatly with the arrival of Iron Age.

Iron's requirement for higher temperature must have been a major disadvantage in a place like the Middle East, where there was a chronic shortage of fuel – a remarkable irony today. Even where fuel was plentiful, iron could not be poured into moulds like bronze – the ancient kiln temperatures did not allow it.

Bronze does not corrode when exposed to moisture. It is less brittle than iron but significantly more brittle than steel. For some centuries, iron was used for ceremonial and ornamental objects before the secret of steel-making was discovered.

The technique relies on a fine balance of actions, which requires a lot of local expertise to perfect. It takes much longer to get enough metal to make a single blade out of steel than out of bronze, and it requires a great deal more skill.

Early Indo-European cultures made a point of excelling in bronze manufacture, and at the turn of the first millennium AD they again spear-headed the transition to steel.

They made a point of being better metal workers that their neighbours, regardless of the terrain. It can be argued that Indo-European smiths enjoyed a certain natural advantage in Arkaim, where the soil is naturally rich in metal ores and, presumably, some kind of fuel for the kilns, possibly wood from the nearby foothills of the Urals. However, this is not true of all terrain conquered and retained by Indo-Europeans. The technological edge was still retained in places such as the Middle East where rival non-Indo-European societies had similar access to natural resources, yet were unable to match their Indo-European neighbours.

The Bible speaks of the Philistines as superior iron workers, who guarded their superiority jealously. At one stage the vanquished Israelites were prohibited to smelt iron and even sharpen iron tools – they were obliged to seek the services of Philistine smiths to maintain their agricultural implements. Clearly, the Israelites had the means to smelt iron – but not so skilfully or ubiquitously as to make control of that activity impossible. According to archaeological record, most contemporary weaponry was bronze, illustrating that steel production was no mean achievement given the conditions in the region.

Yet Philistines did it with relative ease. Likewise, early Iranians, Greeks and Indians were highly skilled metallurgists.

Likewise, the latter Indo-Europeans were the first to adopt firearms and implement them on a systematic basis. The Chinese invented gun powder around 1,000 BC, and they had constructed the first pieces of artillery. Yet five hundred years later Europeans were undisputed masters of this technology. When Turks took Constantinople, they employed German and Genoese artillery engineers, whose handiwork helped shatter the defences first built by Constantine to protect fellow Christians against the pagans.

It is not complicated to group the cited technological characteristics of Indo-Europeans. They all flow from an emphasis on military prowess and technology.

As in the era of diesel-powered chariots, the backbone of Indo-European society was what we now call the military-industrial complex. That handy, if pejorative, Cold War term describes the love triangle between business interests, the military and the political establishment. Money and other currencies of power flow freely between the points of that triangle.

Arguably, the military-industrial complex is not unique to Indo-Europeans, but Indo-European cultures appear to be built around it. It is possible to view their entire social ethos as an extension of this complex.

There is no major European nation that does not have a military-industrial complex. Even peace-loving Sweden makes much profit from manufacturing deadly weapons, used to kill and terrorize far away from the lovely peace of Sweden.

Social characteristics of early Indo-European societies

Furthermore, Indo-Europeans were (and are, to a large extent) characterized by two institutions:

I. A division into hereditary castes, leading to vertical (parent-child) transmission of important areas of expertise, especially that of warriors and priests – a Bronze Age priest also being a scribe, advisor, scientist, physician and legal practitioner.

Even if not exclusively hereditary, these classes handed down a tradition of professionalism. By contrast, other ancient societies nominated military leaders on the basis of birthright rather than expertise, often with disastrous results.

Today we are aghast at the idea of a caste-riven society. There are indeed numerous reasons why this is undesirable in the modern world. We appear to suffer from a chronic shortage of talent in all disciplines, and, if nothing else, the idea of wasting individual potential just because it is inappropriate to one's caste is appalling, not to mention the repugnance of sentencing individuals to circumstances dictated by their parentage.

Alas, ancient reality was very different.

Education (more precisely, vocational training – even today most educational institutions are not in the business of dispensing education) was not a generic commodity, to be purchased off the shelf as it is today. Becoming a physician, a military officer or an architect was not a matter of attending an appropriate course. It was either a case of technical apprenticeship or of learning from expensive mistakes.

It is instantly obvious that a professional guild with hereditary succession represents a major advance in the ability to transmit knowledge. An apprentice who is a blood relative of the master is far likely to be trained better than an apprentice accepted out of institutional considerations.

The caste system is not exclusive to Indo-Europeans, but as with the military-industrial complex, it appears to be a constant and fundamental element of early Indo-European culture. It may be said that castes found in non-Indo-European societies are a result of evolution, a gradual specialization and monopolization of a certain social group (classically, the priesthood or the professional military). In contrast, Indo-Europeans appear to have begun with the caste system a priori.

There are numerous surviving examples of caste structure. To this day, modern Hindus are divided into four categories – the descendants of a military aristocracy, the priests, the merchants and artisans, the peasants. Those who do not fit into either class are discarded as "miscellaneous", an informal fifth class treated as human refuse with no rights of citizenship.

Much reviled, the Indian structure is no more than what occurred in European society until very recently. The European priestly caste was undermined by the split into various learned professions (priests, lawyers, doctors, academics and teachers), but military aristocracy remained the backbone of every European nation until the twentieth century. The world wars had decimated the warrior class, and a new world order deprived it of means to replenish its wealth through plunder.

Whilst no longer hereditary, the warrior class retains its privileged position. Bill Clinton and Lyndon B. Johnson were the only post-war US presidents who has not worn uniforms. A record of distinguished military service remains an important advantage in American elections. Most royal houses of Europe still consider themselves obliged to send at least one son of every generation into military service, even making a point of sending them to live wars.

In Russia the professional military (namely the officer corps, as low-ranking soldiers are temporary conscripts) remains as highly regarded as it was at the time of Lermontov and Tolstoy (both of whom fought in the Caucasus). A military officer is still held up as a guardian of desirable manly values. He commands social standing and personal authority well out of proportion to his income or the nature of his duties.

Ironically, the language base, the most obvious common characteristic of all Indo-Europeans, is the least critical common element. Indo-Europeans would still boast similar results 4,500 years of conquest, whatever language they spoke. The caste system and the military-industrial complex, with a powerful ideological apparatus, were the most obvious secret weapons behind their vast conquests.

The streamlining of these predatory characteristics is not unique to Indo-European cultures. Whether invented independently or copied from Indo-European neighbours, other predators had them too. Indo-Europeans stand out because their success was so much more sustained.

II. Indo-Europeans place a strong emphasis on war, territorial aggression and cultural supremacy, resulting in the erasure of indigenous cultures conquered by Indo-Europeans.

There are two immediately obvious outcomes of this ideology.

First, there is a strong tendency to cultural hegemony, the replacement or modification of the native culture.

 The second element flows from the powerful tendency of the military-industrial complex to subjugate its host society, making war the reason for the state's existence – a nation living to eat, rather than eating to live.

Peaceful forms of mobilization, such as the Egyptian building projects, also have benefits even if they offer no practical return whatsoever. Technology is advanced. Society is economically and socially mobilized (and evidence had long ago dispensed with the myth that the Egyptian pyramids were built by slaves – most of the labourers were, apparently, freeborn men who were respectfully treated by their overseers). Civic order is improved; a nation busily engaged in building canals and pyramids or just attending a religious festival is far less likely to focus on the basic unfairness of life and take their anger out on their rulers– and life in the ancient world could be very unfair indeed. Egyptian and Maya societies both evolved to a great level of sophistication, most probably with a proportional rise in the standard of living, without reliance on war.

However, the return from these benefits is multiplied when social mobilization is coupled to a military one – witness the rapid development of numerous societies throughout history, lately those of England, Germany, France, USSR and USA, not to mention Israel, 40% of whose GNP is spent on defence. The spin-offs for the Israeli education system, technological prowess and military might in terms of bang per unit of hard currency are enormous.

Early Indo-Europeans were no pioneers of ethical thought, as testified by the ancient writings of Hindus and others, who stole enough time from slaughtering their neighbours to leave a written record – the Hittites.

Ancient Hindu epics are works of impressive sophistication and beauty, but they no more instruct the reader in economic sustainability or social justice than they teach nuclear physics. It is possible to scour the early Hindu texts and extract, largely by quoting out of context, passages that suggest a theoretical foundation of a moral system. But there are no Ten Commandments, and there is certainly nothing like Zoroastrian theology that inextricably binds human destiny with the ultimate victory of good over evil.

The Hittite archives, available as a remarkably comprehensive collection of works, portray a society with little concern for human life and far more than a healthy preoccupation with the ability to end life horribly.

The modern trend (that allows the study of Indo-European phenomenon to stay out of controversy) is to downplay the well-documented violence underlying Indo-European cultures, preferring instead to write complex treatises on Proto-Indo-European grave goods. Much of this scholarship consists of bickering over terminology and arguments over rival classification systems of artefacts, belonging to closely related cultures.

It will never be possible to prove whether the so-called Yamna culture represents the archaeological equivalent of Proto-Indo-Europeans. That proposition makes sense, but what matters far more (and receives no academic attention) is the stupendous outcome of Indo-European spread – with the achievements and the damage done along the way.

The pretence is that Indo-European behavioural patterns will go away if we only ignore them. Surely not. Understanding the psychology of a powerful civilization is the only way to deal with its drawbacks. Surely, dealing with the Indo-European impulse to dominate and exterminate begins with the acknowledgement of its existence – but I admit that the logic of political correctness never failed to elude me.

Case study: Bronze-Age Israel

There is no reason not to start with the most controversial scenario to illustrate the advantages of Indo-Europeanization in ancient times – the emergence of Israel as a powerful and successful state in the hotly contested territory of the Fertile Crescent. In the time of King Saul (ruled ?1030 – ?1000 BC) the Israelites were still a mere semi-nomadic rabble, trampled on by powerful Indo-European neighbours, the iron-working, chariot-riding Philistines, who were themselves recent arrivals.

It is believed that they were Greek in origin, survivors of the great war between Egypt and the Sea People, a loose maritime federation of Indo-European fortune seekers similar to Vikings. After the Sea People were defeated, the Egyptians allowed some to settle in the eastern reach of their sphere of influence – Canaan. The Egyptian logic was impeccable, given that a kingdom built by Viking-like cutthroats would serve as an excellent and self-financing guard of the distant eastern frontier.

When David became the second Israelite king (? 1000 BC), that made him a largely nominal leader of a decentralized entity, no more than a loose tribal federation. Indeed, David himself was little more than a commander of a small mercenary force. He left the employ of the very same Philistines a short time before being anointed as king.

Some time after coronation he took Jerusalem, and a radical turn in the Israelite fortunes appears to follow. Within a few short years David's forces subdue the Philistines, who disappeared as a political entity from that point. David went on to thrash and subjugate the Ammonites (the territory of modern Northern Jordan), the Moabites (central Jordan) and the Edomites (southern modern Jordan). The Syrian allies of the Ammonites were defeated when they marched south to intervene. Israel became a small empire in its own right, and it so remained to the end of Solomon's reign (?920 BC).

Even after the split of the kingdom into northern tribes of Israel and a much smaller Jerusalem-centred Judah in the south, the Israelites retained a fearsome military reputation, possessing one of the largest chariot armies in the region for the next century. In 853 BC the Assyrians made their first serious foray into Canaan, and a Canaanite coalition stopped their advance in a battle at Karkar (modern Lebanon), to which Ahab, the king of the northern Israelite kingdom, sent a large chariot (!) force.

Was that meteoric ascent due to natural maturation of a militant people, who finally developed sufficient expertise in warfare to best their powerful neighbours? Possible, but improbable. The impetus for Israelites to undergo such a transformation was surely greater a century before, when Philistines wreaked havoc with their lives at will.

There is another explanation. One of the more coherent theories about ethnicity of pre-Davidic occupants of Jerusalem suggests that the so-called Jebusites were a Hurrian trade colony, an outpost that was probably ceded to David by arrangement.

The Hurrians were a people whose homeland lay north-west of Mesopotamia. They were a Middle Eastern people ruled by an Indo-European elite from around 1500 BC. They had a complicated genetic relationship with their more famous neighbours, the Hittites. It cannot be described in simple X conquered Y terms, being more like the political and cultural relationship between Korea and Japan. The Hittites may have received their Indo-European culture from an early invasion by Mittani, an Indo-European dynasty who ruled Hurrians. As centuries went on, the Hurrian kingdom weakened and was conquered by the Hittites (and finally destroyed by their southern neighbours, the Assyrians).

In any case, the two neighbouring powers may be grouped into a single cultural sphere. Outsiders easily confused the Hurrians and the Hittites, just as a native of a German colony, such as Papua New Guinea, was hard-put to tell the difference between a Bavarian and a Berliner.

Although both the Hurrian states and the Hittite empire were long-eclipsed by the time of David's ascendancy, the Hurrians/Hittites were still around, often as isolated settlements that possibly functioned in the same manner as white-run Rhodesia or as British-run Hong Kong.

The Bible does not mention any great fighting during the conquest of Jerusalem, which remained an independent island in a sea of Israelite territory. That reported lack of gore stands in stark contrast to other Israelite victories in Canaan.

Jerusalem (*Yerushalaim* in Hebrew) was not *Yir Shalom*, the City of Peace – a ridiculous notion at any phase of its history. *Yir* is Hebrew for city, and there would have been no second vowel in *Yerushalaim.* For instance, Armageddon is *Yir Megiddo* – the city of *Megiddo.*

Rather, *Yerushalaim* was *Ir Hasalem*, the city of Salem – the moon god (also the god of dusk) of the Hurrians.

David supposedly took this impregnable stronghold by leading his assault force via an aqueduct, a natural passage in the bedrock under the city that leads to a spring. That tunnel has now been excavated, and it could indeed be used to infiltrate the hilltop fortified as ancient Jerusalem from outside.

If one is to take the story verbatim, the defenders did not adequately guard or reinforce that portal, even though David was clearly on the prowl in their neighbourhood.

Given what we know about the military expertise of the Hurrians, that is exceptionally unlikely – being an obvious weak point of an otherwise impregnable fortress, the aqueduct would be thoroughly fortified (which archaeological evidence shows clearly). Any attack through the aqueduct would be easily repelled: the assailants would have to ascend through a narrow tunnel, no more than two abreast. The defenders waiting for them above would slash the advance party into mince, and the passage would soon be barricaded with corpses. Meanwhile, the noise would rouse defenders in large numbers, and the attack could not possibly succeed.

Yet the Bible reports David's assault as successful. This very much suggests a political compromise in which the Jebusites (or, perhaps, one faction in the city) allowed David through the aqueduct on purpose.

In all likelihood, the inhabitants of a far-flung Hurrian outpost realized that their days as independent enclave were drawing to an end, the military superiority of their ancient culture no longer being sufficient to offset dwindling numbers. They picked David, the most successful robber baron of the region, to annexe their city – possibly without the knowledge, or even against the will of the majority. A small assault team was allowed to gain entry, and, once they were inside, their presence was presented as a fait accompli, a pretext to end further resistance.

There are further indications in the Bible that the native population of Jerusalem remained intact and lived in harmony with invaders. It would have taken David little time to understand the value of the administrative apparatus and other institutions maintained by his new subjects. A talented leader and organizer, he may well have calculated all this beforehand.

That would also explain the tolerance of idol worship, retained in Judah for centuries after David, and the cultural divide between Jerusalem and the rest of Israel, where the population was less influenced by fusion with Indo-European society.

Much as their presence riled the Israelite clergy, Hurrian priests were too valuable to simply crush or drive underground. Like all priestly orders of the ancient (and not-so-ancient) world, they were also librarians, archivists, historians, political advisors, scientists, economists, engineers, agronomists, doctors and administrators.

Then we have a matter-of-fact mention of a Hurrian (as noted, Hittites and Hurrans were often confused by outsiders), clearly a high-ranking officer, serving under David. Uriah, called "the Hittite" in the Bible, was Bathsheba's unfortunate first husband. The name "Uriah" is a crude ethnicity-based pseudonym like "Ivan" or "Fritz", referring to the man's origin. In all probability the Israelite chroniclers didn't exert themselves to reproduce his real name, which may have been a polysyllabic epic like Supilluliuma.

Uriah's status and the manner of his personal interaction with David (when the king is not busy seducing Uriah's wife) indicate that Uriah's allegiance was trusted absolutely. He was no mere mercenary, owning a house in easy sight of the royal palace, and the Machiavellian manner of his assassination was not only noticed, but considered a grave offence. The popular king is denounced by the resident arbiter of good manners, and he is punished by divine wrath, through the death of his first child by Uriah's hapless widow.

For all the reputed righteousness of David's kingdom, it is difficult to see how in those coarse times so much fuss would result from the killing of a foreign hireling – who was, after, all, a professional soldier. The likes of Uriah died like flies.

A ready alternative explanation is that Uriah was no foreigner but a native citizen of Jerusalem, whose fate very much mattered to his fellow natives.

All of this suggests a peaceful annexation of Jerusalem – it is most unlikely that members of a population vanquished in a violent conquest would be trusted to command troops shortly afterwards, or that a woman of hostile stock would be permitted to bring up the next king – the second child of David by Bathsheba not only lived but succeeded David.

Solomon the half-Hurrian was even named after Salem (in Hebrew Solomon is pronounced as *Shlomoh*, literally "Of Salem", or "Son of Salem"). Again, this is nothing to do with the sentiment of modern *Shalom* – what warrior king would call his son "Peacenik"? *Shlomoh* is not even Solomon's real name – which was Jedidiah, Hebrew for friend of Yahweh. It seems that he took the trouble to be known as Son of Salem some time in his early, undocumented life as a barely known junior prince, struggling for relevance in a court filled with equally desperate half-brothers.

Israelite generals, prior to and including David, were amateurs, sometimes talented but usually short of that mark. They may be better described as "reserve" officers, and their performance can be best described as hit and miss. That was the norm in most (non-Indo-European) societies of the region. Having a professional officer corps always made an enormous difference – witness the success of Jordan's Arab Legion, a Bedouin infantry commanded by mercenary British officers – the only credible opponent that modern Israel had to face in all of its wars.

The assault on Jerusalem appears to be David's last action as a commander. He continued to lead troops into battle when he was anointed as king. But after the conquest of Jerusalem David assumes a strictly political role. Even during a civil war, waged by professional troops on both sides, David refrains from assuming personal command, even as his life is threatened by an imminent defeat of loyal troops.

One explanation for this is that the character of his army has changed after the takeover of Jerusalem. David no longer considered his experience of twenty years as a commander of mercenary tribesmen relevant to the new military.

That hypothesis explains why the Israelites suddenly proceeded to trounce their long-standing enemy, the Philistines: they were now run by professional civilian administrators. Their army was trained and commanded by a corps of hereditary officers, and its weaponry was upgraded to a standard set by a millennium of accumulated expertise, supplied by experienced professionals who aligned their survival with David's ascendancy.

The Kurgan Hypothesis

Modern anthropology offers one an easy career path. All one needs to do is to restate, in more or less own words, that Indo-Europeans were bad, violent people with ugly male tendencies and a lack of ecological awareness.

These villains, one has to enlarge, had massacred an eco-wise, matriarchal, socially just society that was guided by female deities (a supposition based on genital imagery, real and imagined, in pre-Indo-European artefacts). One also needs to conclude that the pre-Indo-European population of Eurasia led an idyllic, politically correct existence, which simply did not require technical progress. Ergo, everything that happened after the Indo-European invasion was bad.

The high priestess of this school is the late Marija Gimbutas, a Lithuanian-born Californian anthropologist who was a formidable expert on late Neolithic artefacts of Eastern Europe.

In the scientific phase of her life Gimbutas formulated the most commonly accepted hypothesis about the Indo-European expansion. She probably wasn't the first scholar to voice it, but she can be mostly credited with giving that view substance through her expertise in East European prehistory.

She placed the origin of Indo-Europeans in a rather narrow region in the Pontic steppe, some five hundred kilometres to the north of the Caspian Sea. Gimbutas earned her place in history by postulating (before it was possible to confirm this with population genetics) that Indo-European spread constituted a cultural, rather than genetic, change.

However, her greatest fame stems from the last decade of her life, when she abandoned her scholarly robes for the shapeless sack-cloth of eco-feminism. The ensuing product, collectively labelled as "feminist archaeology", ranks with the Nazis "Jewish Physics" (referring to quantum mechanics, which the Nazis banned), or Soviet "Marxist-Leninist biology" (which saw bizarre and disastrous agricultural experiments, based on irrational theories).

Sadly, Gimbutas was allowed to thrive in her pseudo-scientific tangent, encountering only half-hearted opposition from serious academics.

Returning to her scientific phase, Gimbutas named the original, Proto-Indo-Europeans the Kurgan culture (*kurgan* being a borrowed Turkic word in Russian, meaning an earth mound in the steppe). Kurgans nearly always mark the sites of ancient burials prevalent in the steppes of Southern Russia.

Gimbutas' Kurgan people correspond to the

Proto-Indo-Europeans of modern science. From the beginning she portrayed them as successful thugs. From there it was not a long leap to the fairy tale about a matriarchal paradise, which the decidedly male thugs had vandalized and replaced with a destructive juggernaut – one that eventually put Russian nuclear reactors in Gimbutas' native Lithuania.

Albeit poisoning the occasional harvest, the said reactors nevertheless shield her relatives from cold and famine. Their American counterparts fuel Gimbutas' means of disseminating her opinion to the entire world, being part of a sophisticated civilization that preserves her pearls for future admirers, equally ungrateful for being dragged out of caves.

What this proves is that anthropology had learnt nothing from the Mead fiasco: feminist archaeology is nothing more than a coherently articulated myth, authored by a scientist who discarded her duty to science and chose instead to damage it with muddled personal beliefs.

An essential element to her hypothesis is the assertion that pre-Indo-European societies were good because they were run by women, who were revered and worshipped because of their obvious superiority. Gimbutas rests the former assertion on the profuse presence of the female form in Neolithic art, including some obscure symbols like triangles, V-shapes and other possible symbols of female genitalia.

A visitor to any public toilet will attest that female genital imagery is as abundant today as it was in pre-Indo-European societies. Nevertheless, no one would suggest that its prevalence implies a worship of, or even a basic respect for, women, by either the artist or his audience.

Even a generous critic would concur that images in modern public conveniences are not of a high artistic standard. Nevertheless, the perpetrators are quite able to portray their subject matter, leaving lamentably little room for ambiguity.

It is not likely that Neolithic pornographers were any less talented, and they were probably far more familiar with their subject matter. If they cared to scratch images of the vulva into rock, there was no reason for them to obfuscate, by drawing triangles bisected with straight lines or dots aligned in triangular pattern.

The sexist content of Gimbutas' views alone should have rendered them ineligible for serious discussion. If she believed that a world run by women was free of violence and domination, she clearly never experienced an all-female environment. A stint in any convent, boarding school or a female prison would have her rethink her thesis.

The people Indo-Europeans had vanquished left

plentiful evidence that they were as violent and politically incorrect as could be imagined – as are surviving Stone Age people today. A modern observer will find precious little charm in the social dynamic of primitive cultures, especially when it comes to the treatment of women.

Many prehistoric societies were indeed matrilineal, but that is quite different to a matriarchy. Matrilinearity is natural in a clan environment, where sex between different individuals occurs at random times.

Nothing else is random about the sexual hierarchy of a primate pack: the most aggressive male is the boss and has first call on all the ladies. The most attractive females are reserved for his exclusive use, whereas others are available to all males. Unless the pack is reduced to critically low numbers, there is no ready way for a male to distinguish his offspring from other children in the pack.

Unlike other apes, humans do not restrict intercourse to periods of fertility, making it even harder for a successful inseminator to identify his progeny. On the other hand, everyone knows who gave birth to whom – and it is the mother who secures the child's identity and survival.

That results in women having the traditional monopoly on early child rearing, boys reaching a certain age relocated to the male side of pack.

Whilst that necessarily has implications for the mother's role in the child's identity, single motherhood, as its modern practitioners can attest, hardly places women into a superior position.

There is one fact that can be quoted in support of the feminist distaste for Indo-European cultures – the nastiness that they lavish on women.

Early militaristic societies would have had no use for women, other than as incubators and beasts of burden. Even when the development of the recurving bow equalled the opportunity between sexes in war, the hardships of ancient warfare greatly favoured those with greater strength and size.

It is not surprising, therefore, that early Indo-Europeans treated women worse than other contemporary cultures. Amongst the earliest documented Indo-European cultures women are very much a property of their father or husband, lower than a male slave – who,, if nothing else, generally had some expectation of decent treatment as a valuable piece of equipment. Indo-European women appear to have been regarded as expendable, with women in high office few and far in between. The middle castes – warriors, priests and artisans – are exclusively male, their wives being mere chattels.

Modern India, a society with the longest

continuous tradition since the Indo-European arrival, has only recently cracked down on the practice of *suttee.* The widow is expected to join her deceased husband on the funeral pyre, despite being very much alive and, usually, without being an opportunity to voice her thoughts on the matter.

There is plenty of evidence about where that tradition came from – it is common to find the remains of husband and wife in the graves of prehistoric Eurasians. Needless to say, they did not die simultaneous deaths naturally – these are not the hasty burials of plague victims but carefully arranged inhumations. The grave goods include the deceased's favourite females, who, when the state of preservation permits, carry marks of being brutally murdered.

In the modern age it is especially easy to empathize with Gimbutas, who fled her native Lithuania during World War II. The tiny Baltic states enjoyed a brief period of independence from Russia since the Bolshevik Revolution and subsequent Civil War (1917-1922), which resulted in Russia becoming too weak to reassert control of former provinces.

From 1940 these countries were occupied by Soviet and German armies in quick succession. Whilst Soviet troops occupied the Baltic region without actual combat, what followed was a bloodbath of monumental proportions.

Paramilitary (*NKVD*, or ministry of the interior) troops proceeded to "neutralize the ruling class" (anyone with civil authority or tertiary education). The victims were rounded up and murdered, often horrifically, in local jails.

When the Nazis occupied all three Baltic states a few months later, they made a point of allowing the natives to view the Soviet handiwork, and few came away unchanged.

I once interviewed a witness who was a young woman at the time. She made the mistake of venturing out to help her neighbours search for the corpses of their loved ones in Riga's central prison. What she described still gives me nightmares two decades later.

It is not surprising that there was a strong sympathy with the Nazis in the Baltic region, despite their extermination campaign against Jews, Gypsies, nationalists and communists.

Lithuania was again occupied by Soviet troops at the end of the war. The carnage resumed, now targeting Nazi sympathizers as well as nationalists, who were now organized as guerilla units. Sporadic armed resistance to the Soviet occupation continued until mid-1960's.

Both the Nazi and the Soviet regimes were terrifying monsters, qualitatively different to "typical" Indo-European conquerors such as the Romans or the British. The nakedness of totalitarian bestiality intensified the shock of World War II – both regimes prided themselves on mass murder and, upon taking new territory, performed mass murder in plain sight of the population as a terror tactic.

Having witnessed and probably narrowly survived these unthinkable events, Gimbutas would have been desperate to believe that what she saw is not the ultimate result of civilization. Like many fellow witnesses of that war, she would grasp at any suggestion that humanity was not always homicidal. That monstrous regimes and wars are a derangement imposed on humanity by cultural conditioning. That social progress does more than provide a more efficient means of mass murder.

World war (the second, arguably, being a resumption of the first) proved a pivotal event in the way many Europeans view the world. Three generations on, they desperately want to believe that a non-violent world was possible once and is therefore possible again. It is understandable – to quote Einstein, one does not know what weapons will be used in a third world war, but only sticks and stones will be possible in the fourth.

One can equally understand how Margaret Mead, a product of a generation that practised extreme sexual repression, would be seduced by tales of free love. Growing up as a presumably healthy young woman, she must have bitterly resented the senseless curtailment of her normal drives. She would have been intoxicated by a vision of a Pacific utopia where copulation is free of consequences – and, being sexually naïve, Mead failed to take into account such things as unwanted pregnancy, sexual abuse or sexually transmitted infections – which famously savaged the Pacific population in the past two centuries.

The society Indo-Europeans replaced was not better morally or ecologically. Archaeological evidence is quite unequivocal about the natives of Europe prior to Indo-European invasion: mass graves with skeletons showing evidence of violent death indicate that genocide is not an Indo-European invention.

Nevertheless, Indo-Europeans rode over them, barely stopping to mop up resistance.

The long-term consequences of a culture dedicated to and capable of such conquests are not hard to imagine even today, as we try to fathom the Indo-European spread before the era of internal combustion and automatic weapons.

Zarathushtra, however, witnessed the dawn of the chariot age first-hand. In contrast to the priests of modern political correctness, he understood the problem completely, as do most witnesses and narrow survivors of such events.

But in contrast to most before and after himself, he offered a simple solution to the central dilemma of the Kurgan culture. Zoroastrianism promotes a life of productivity as an honourable alternative to glory through conquest and bloodshed:

Put down fury, check violence, you who wish to strengthen the promotion of good mind through righteousness because a forward-looking man is dedicated to this.

(Gathas: xiii)

Zarathushtra preached sublimation – diversion of war-like tendencies away from destruction. He taught his followers to fight more abstract enemies instead of neighbours – crime, sloth, disorder, hunger and other forms of resource mismanagement.

There is a modern example of such sublimation. A certain nation (which is not Indo-European) used to regard bloodshed as ultimate glory. For many centuries its elite was so desperate to perpetrate murder and mayhem that it ladled them out in their own country, not even bothering to travel elsewhere. The result was a thousand years of constant war.

Eventually, that nation collided with Indo-Europeans. It faithfully copied Indo-European ways and immediately embarked on a campaign of regional expansion using modern Indo-European technology and methods. It trounced every opponent until it bit off more than it could chew, attacking three Indo-European powers at once.

After a brief but painful re-education at the hands of these enemies, the said nation did a remarkable job of retooling its military-industrial machine for peaceful manufacture. Its social ethos was restyled to cater to sustainability and productivity instead of combat and glorious death.

In the past the proud cutthroats of that nation would sooner suicide than engage in any peaceful and productive occupation. Yet their descendants are now running high-technology production lines with the fanaticism once reserved for running at enemy lines with broken swords.

Within three generations "Made in Japan" became the hallmark of ultimate quality and dedication to perfection. Japanese goods are prized in every market. The resultant wealth, which Japan carefully accumulated, allowed the Japanese to buy the nations that their grandfathers tried to conquer.

The national ethos of modern Japan bears remarkable similarities to Zarathushtra's vision: productivity, neatness, respect for public order, a powerful individual discipline and dedication to the common good.

I am not suggesting that post-war Japan was

reconstructed along Zoroastrian lines by deliberate design. It simply learned a bitter lesson about thuggery – that there is always a bigger thug – and arrived at Zarathushtra's conclusions from there. Only three generations after the last warlords, Japan is a highly successful society, having won a great victory in the metaphysical war against disorder.

That victory is cause for hope.

Kurgan Culture in the Americas – a case study of Indo-European expansion

In his excellent book "In Search of Indo-Europeans" J. P. Mallory states that one is embarrassed to talk about marauding horsemen from the Pontic steppe – for fear of ridicule.

With great respect to this scholar of rare integrity, ridicule by orthodox practitioners should be something of a badge of honour in any controversial discipline. As per the Margaret Mead story, ridicule by the establishment should be an incentive to continue along the same line of reasoning.

Using Occam's Razor, one may suggest that the rampaging horsemen are not only a plausible mechanism of Indo-European expansion, but the best explanation. There is no reason why prehistoric Indo-Europeans should have behaved differently from their descendants, as portrayed at the dawn of recorded history by the likes of Homer.

Ancient people were no less capable than their modern descendants. In fact, savage selection may have created greater abilities than the competition-phobic reality of the present. Today we take for granted the images of Romans rampaging in Minor Asia and North Africa,

Mongols rampaging all over Eurasia, conquistadors rampaging all over the Americas, Nazi rampaging all over Europe. Why not Proto-Indo-Europeans?

Why, other than for political correctness, would anyone assert that the ancestors of these conquerors stopped at borders and applied for permanent residency?

The collapse of pre-Columbian American cultures is well-documented, for it occurred in relatively recent times and at the hands of a literate society. The conquest of the Americas is not as well-documented as some other such exploits, but there is no dispute about the general flow of events. There was a frontal assault on a quilt work of weak nations by an aggressor with technological superiority that compensated for minuscule numbers. The conquered nations were forced to convert to the culture and language of their invader.

The Mayans and the Aztecs were no strangers to war. For all their technical and artistic prowess, their religious and political practices appear to have consisted of continuous, abattoir-like spillage of human life, in which wars were an important source of sacrificial victims. Yet their armies caved in when confronted by tiny Spanish war bands.

This feat owes little to firearms, which were

more of a hindrance than help at that stage of their evolution. A far more relevant factor in the Spanish victory is the horse – an old ally of rampaging Indo-Europeans, the original vehicle of a quality blitzkrieg. Another relevant factor is another traditional tool, steel. The third factor is professional military training. The proficiency shown by Spanish commanders rested on three millennia of accumulated expertise, hard-won knowledge of blitzkrieg campaigns than now covered much of the globe.

A cultural genocide followed physical slaughter. Native Americans who resisted in any way were massacred. This was provoked at every opportunity, as a deliberate tactic to tilt the numbers in favour of Spanish colonists. Both forms of genocide succeeded almost entirely and in the space of a few generations – a remarkable fact considering the ratio of natives to invaders and the vast territory in question – only in extremely difficult terrain did native culture manage to survive.

What happened in Spanish Americas cannot prove what took place all over Eurasia 4,500 years ago, but it shows that the Gimbutas model works. Violent rampage, reign of terror, demolition of native culture and social structure allow minimal number of invaders to succeed – and it is not as if the Spanish adventure is the only recorded cataclysm of such magnitude and speed.

Alexander and Hitler achieved most victories with relatively little physical destruction or even resistance, their invasions rapidly covering vast stretches of territory. Alexander destroyed a handful of cities, mainly after fierce resistance, but in his latter campaigns his reputation went before him and saved him much effort. Most of the destruction of World War II was actually incurred when Germans were evicted from occupied territories.

If Indo-Europeans were peaceful migrants, like Russian Jews who worked their way from the Bronx sweatshops to Wall Street, why is Indo-European epos entirely devoted to violent conquest? Why did Indo-European smiths perfect weapons, rather than agricultural implements? Why didn't they spread other technologies – agriculture, maritime navigation, astronomy, cloth weaving or sensuous poetry? Why is it instead that to this day, any Indo-European society of consequence is still run by the military-industrial complex?

An unbiased observer using common sense will conclude that Gimbutas got it right in her pre-feminist phase. Proto-Indo-Europeans appear to have moved with the same speed as more recent invaders, but in such small numbers that they left little physical evidence of their movements. The same observer will hasten, to add, however, that their cultural legacy is undeniable and its sheer geographic span speaks for itself.

The relative proportion of carrot and stick – violent subjugation and coercion versus seduction with superior standard of living – would have varied in each case. Likewise, the cultural exchange was not all one-way. We know that some primitive Indo-European societies, upon invasion, assumed many cultural characteristics of those they subjugated – for instance, the Hittites adopted many conventions of the older Hurrian civilization, and Crusaders assimilated into the Arab lifestyle, and they took it back to Europe after eviction from the Middle East.

Taking away the dross from what Gimbutas said later, one quickly comes to the conclusion that she was right about a few things. She did not deny that Indo-Europeans were history's greatest catalyst. She admitted that in Eurasia their assault on the eco-paradise of their neighbours put an end to a million years of Stone Age and began recorded history.

Indo-Europeans may or may not have ruined a politically correct matriarchal Eden, but their propensity for taking what is not theirs and relishing the resultant mayhem is undeniable.

It takes nothing more than a spin of the globe to see that the story of Indo-Europeans constitutes the most important chapter in the history of humanity. The rest consists of chapters about cultures who rode Indo-European coattails, such as the Jews, and much shorter chapters about others, such as Carthaginians, who made the mistake of standing in the way.

Global domination – the failed contenders

China remains the only major cultural bloc that developed next to, but in splendid insulation from Indo-Europeans. It is the only bloc that Indo-European culture failed to infiltrate (in the strict sense of the word) and remould unto its image, arguably to this day. There were plenty of contacts between China and its Indo-European neighbours: for instance, during the time of Parthia so many Parthians emigrated to China that the Chinese even evolved a convention of naming them with a prefix *An*. But they did not alter the basic Chinese culture.

In recent times the Chinese deigned to copy some "long-nose" habits and techniques, very much for the purpose of beating the Europeans at most of their own games. But Chinese society remains essentially Chinese, despite a period of occupation by Indo-European powers. In particular, it steadfastly refuses to practise violent imperialism: its heroes wear business suits and factory overalls, not the mention lab coats. Chinese civilization appears to have "grown out" of the expansionist mentality early in its development, and Mao's attempt at militarizing its ethos along Soviet lines was a notable failure.

China once nominally ruled and exerted cultural

hegemony throughout a vast territory, which encompassed the modern Indochina, Mongolia, Korea and Japan. But it showed no appetite for further expansion and maintained peaceful relations with its neighbours until the twentieth century. Plagued by population pressure, Mao briefly toyed with the notion of wresting the mostly empty Siberia from Russia. Fortunately for the Chinese people, their leader abandoned that plan in the nick of time.

Many non-Indo-European adventurers practised aggression just as well if not better – but the global village of today is neither Assyrian nor Semitic, nor Mongolian.

The common feature of all these forgotten conquerors leaps one in the eye: they did not force their culture on conquered people. The Assyrians, for instance, were interested only in tribute, otherwise having little contact with those they conquered, presumably in anticipation of having to annihilate them when they eventually rebelled. There was not the slightest attempt to export Assyrian culture or religion.

Assyrians are an interesting example – in viciousness and military effectiveness they were as good as any Indo-Europeans before or since. They had extensive contacts with Indo-European Mittani and their cultural relatives, the Hittites. It is possible that Assyrians copied elements of Indo-European power structure (for instance, a standing army) and military expertise (especially the chariot doctrine) from their Indo-European neighbours. But what they failed to emulate is the cultural aggression – possibly because the neighbouring Mittani elite did not practise this themselves. Indeed, the Mittani slowly assimilated into the native Hurrian culture.

Whatever the reasons, Assyrians were not cultural hegemonists. They thought of themselves as predatory overlords of surrounding nations. Their empire progressed in stops and starts, not even a pale imitation of the Indo-European explosion.

There was no technical reason for this, looking at the problem from an Indo-European point of view: Assyrians could field much greater numbers than Alexander. Their military technology and discipline were better than that of Cyrus, who destroyed the capital of their collapsed empire and conquered a much larger territory around their former borders. Assyrians didn't flinch from any bestiality, which they applied with equal relish to their citizens – their law reads more like a cheap horror novel than a legal codex.

Assyrians collapsed under the blows of hateful neighbours, who gradually recovered from Assyrian thrashings and regrouped out of Assyrian reach. Persians saw no reason for restraint when they destroyed Nineveh – after centuries of cohabitation, they regarded Assyria as nothing other than a venomous pest.

Egypt, that favourite uncle of early civilization, was quite content to ignore the outside world most of the time. It failed to take advantage of the opportunities afforded along the coast of North Africa, and it failed to advance into the sub-Saharan region, where it would have encountered little credible opposition. It eventually expanded into Canaan, only to create a buffer zone out of expendable client states.

The reward for that policy came without warning. A storm of chariot-driving Hyksos invaders burst into Egypt from Asia. The Hyksos, who sound very much like Anatolian Indo-Europeans (their origin has not been ascertained), had crushed Egyptian armies and set up a rival kingdom in the Nile delta, forcing the sovereign Egyptian state upriver. Egypt had to learn many humiliating lessons before it was able to match the barbarians in battle and evict the Hyksos at long last – six generations of Egyptians lived in a culture on the brink of extinction.

After Egypt was reunified, it enjoyed something of an expansionary phase, mainly reconquering adjacent territories lost during the Hyksos period. Thereafter it returned to bad habits – reviving a closeted culture that held anything foreign in contempt. The result was a gradual dissipation of economic vigour and military strength, then invasions that damaged the sovereign state beyond repair. They were two raids from Assyria that opened the way for colonization by Persia. Finally, the Graeco-Roman era saw a marked displacement of the original traditions, religion and language.

No one speaks the language of ancient Egypt apart from the Coptic minority. Its religion has disappeared. Its written legacy was found and deciphered only by sheer luck. Some echoes of ancient Egypt remain in modern Judaism: circumcision, prohibition on uttering the name of God and recitation "Amen" (Amon being the Egyptian sun god). Otherwise, all traces of this very old civilization are gone, and it is only known to the public due to the hard work of modern archaeologists.

Phoenicians built an empire out of maritime colonies, scattered around the Mediterranean basin. These colonies appear to have existed in near-total cultural isolation from the natives; there is no suggestion that Phoenicians attempted to spread their culture. The emphasis was on trade and symbiosis rather than tribute or direct rule, the colonies being thoughtfully positioned entrepôts for such trade.

The colonists did not have direct control over their hinterland. It is unlikely that even the land on which Phoenicians colonies were built was seized by force. It was certainly protected by military superiority of the colonists, but force was not used to spread the Phoenician way of life. The natives retained their power structure, language and culture, whatever the precise power balance with the colonists.

One can argue that the downfall of the Phoenician empire came precisely from this arrangement. Phoenicians were always a minority in lands occupied by their native populations, and relationships oscillated between wary symbiosis and resentment.

Because Phoenicians relied on neighbours to supply military muscle, it is no surprise that they were defeated as soon as the enemy offered the natives a better deal. It was in this manner that Carthage lost her Spanish domain, and it was also in this manner that Hannibal was finally defeated by a Roman army – the defection of an influential Lybian chief deprived Hannibal of his cavalry wing. That proved pivotal at the battle of Zama, which ended Hannibal as a credible threat to Rome.

Possibly motivated by Zoroastrian ideals, Achaemenid Persians did not force their ways on conquered nations and practised official tolerance of all religions and cultures. It can be argued that their empire fell apart precisely because of its cultural diversity. Multinational Persian armies looked and behaved like a horde of football fans at a world championship. There was little coordination in the deployment of different contingents, who came in variable numbers, brought weapons of their choice and fought in their own way under a loose central command.

The Greeks, whose weapons and tactics were rigorously standardized, mowed down the Persians with ease. They were outnumbered only as blades of a lawn mower are outnumbered by blades of grass. The only real opposition came from the Immortals, an elite corps of mainly Persian infantry, whose weapons, tactics and command were up to the Greek standard.

One concludes that empires tolerant of cultural diversity are relatively short-lived. Further reflection suggests that aggression and cultural genocide are crimes that pay.

Invaders who merely shake down the conquered for money are forgotten as soon as their powers ebb. But if they take the trouble to force the natives to adopt their ways, especially if they come to share language and religion, the conquered people have little choice but become natural allies of the invader.

This irony is lived out in many places today – the former servants get on with their former colonial masters better than they do with neighbouring nations. The former masters also make handsome profits, selling their former servants shoddy goods that would never sell in a competitive market, such as second-rate arms and overpriced civil engineering contracts.

Former servants maintain close political relations – which, speaking logically, should be eternally cold because of past wrongs. This happens even when the former colonial power lies a world away and wields none of its former influence on the world stage.

This was possibly the most significant innovation of Proto-Indo-Europeans as they set out on their global conquest – erasure of native culture works better than ongoing military intimidation. Driven, possibly, by the same supremacist ideology that drives cultural genocide today, Indo-Europeans forced their culture on those they conquered – and that is why these nations remain Indo-European today. A system of carrots and sticks resulted in subject people become Hellenized, Romanized, Anglicized, Russified, Latinized – converted and turned away from their roots. Like Jews and North American Indians, many natives resisted, but only succeeded in provoking a bloodbath.

Indo-Europeans – the winning formula

We can now assemble the model of Indo-European success:

- A culture that glorifies war and seemingly meaningless destruction.

- An economy tooled to service the military machine, with exploitation of all available resources by the military apparatus.

- The latter, in turn, rolls over the neighbours and returns with the spoils – the dividends of expansionism to which society rapidly becomes addicted.

- The vanquished are converted to Indo-European culture through a carrot and stick approach. The carrot is (in many cases) a superior standard of living, and the stick either forces the natives into Indo-European practices on pain of death, as in Judea under the Seleucid Greeks, or reduces non-compliers to second-rate citizens, such as the Muslim subjects of the Russian Empire.

- Apart from being relatively sustainable, the structure is economically and psychologically addictive. Instead of emphasis on productivity and sustainability as advocated by Zarathushtra, the classic Indo-European ethos plays on the worst instincts of the human psyche. A society of warriors fed and otherwise served by captured slaves is much easier to sell to the public than a society of Amish-style toilers.

A culture is an entity called a meme. This is a relatively new concept, which boils down to a model of ideas and cultures competitively reproducing themselves just like genetic information. Memes are information constructs transmitted by biological matter (until computers begin to invent viable memes), with the most successful meme being the most prolific. Religions, cultures, cults and fashions are all memes – they survive by self-spread.

Reproductive success means precisely that – it does not imply that the successful outcome is also the most desirable in the long run. Bipolar disease (previously known as manic depression) is very common (around 2.5% in any population), despite its sufferers ranging from mildly impaired to severely dysfunctional. But one feature of bipolar disease is a greatly increased sex drive. Sufferers therefore reproduce far out of proportion to their social or economic status.

Genes do not care what results from their reproduction. It is not important whether or not the carrier of genes enjoys their success – all that matters is whether the genes are passed on.

Likewise, memes don't care for the consequences of their spread. We don't need to like Indo-European culture, its methods or its legacy. But we do need to acknowledge is its success.

From an evolutionary point of view, the spread of Indo-European culture makes it the most successful meme in history.

Since the Nazi rampage we were brought up not to say such things, but that doesn't make them untrue. Nor, indeed, does it mean that the Nazi meme was superior to that of its victims – it too failed the test of survival.

One can summarize with the obvious statement – the Indo-European meme is particularly successful in exploiting elements of collective human behaviour. It does not contain any unique elements. It is the combination of these elements, especially the military-industrial complex and a war ethos going back into prehistory, which proved a winner – a crudely formed key that happens to be the best match to the lock. Contained by that lock is the violent genie of primate psyche.

We have to get over the distaste for the unpalatable past and present. Perhaps, if we study them with enough objectivity, even more distasteful developments may be avoided in the future.

There is a lot at stake, for in the thermonuclear age the lock, to which the Indo-European culture constitutes the best-matching key, holds closed the box of Pandora.

Experts versus reality

Alas, you would be hard-pressed to divine the importance of the Indo-European phenomenon from the works of authorities in Indo-European studies.

Instead, you will find a bewildering kaleidoscope of prehistoric cultures known only by bewildering names of locations and burial contents. If one wanted to deliberately obfuscate the golden thread of truth, he could do no better than unleash a torrent of terms like Andronovo Culture (after the village in which the first of typical remains were found), Corded Ware Culture (distinguished by rope indentations in hand-shaped pottery), Afanasyevo Culture (location), Yamna Culture (*yamnaya* being Russian for "belonging to the pit"). Archaeology could badly do with a revised classification, hopefully based on something more logical like coordinates and dates.

This accrued mess steers the newcomer from a sad fact: the prehistoric world will always remain that – prehistoric, understood only in broad terms and with much vital information irretrievably lost. To quote Leonardo da Vinci, when most people die, they leave behind only full toilets. There is a very profound limitation on what can be learned about them many centuries later.

It seems that in archaeology a thesis is a mere

matter of defining a new culture by pointing out some ways in which it may be distinct from its geographic and chronological neighbours. Alas, this is seldom a productive outcome.

The argument of how archaeological findings reflect genuine cultural differences is as old as time. It is worth giving an example that illustrates this dilemma.

Imagine future archaeologists, busy digging up twentieth century car dumps. This will no doubt provide employment for generations of social scientists. No doubt they will begin earnestly, identifying the twentieth century horizon (a broad spectrum of contemporary cultures), its common feature being vehicles with four wheels and an internal combustion engine.

Then, however, we may see the definition of a Toyota culture as distinct, perhaps, from a Land Rover culture. This is not a very rigorous classification, as it does not correspond to genuinely different cultures. Land Rover was evicted from its unique niche by Toyota in a relatively short period, and this did not happen because of a change such as adoption of Japanese culture – Toyota products merely proved more reliable. Drivers of either vehicle still speak the same language, drive in the same manner and live the same lifestyle – although, perhaps, Land Rover owners devote more of their time to towing and repairing their vehicles.

But another future archaeologist, perhaps finding it difficult to cling to his profession, might extend the classification by dividing the twentieth century horizon into White Vehicle Culture and Coloured Vehicle Culture. He may even get away with it.

If so, another talent longing for recognition may build a career by defining the Ferromagnetic Culture (vehicles with cassette players), as distinct from the Laser Culture (vehicles with CD players). All being well, speculation about the differences between these will translate into a paperback with a humble preface and a lifetime tenure at some leafy American college.

Whilst such activities may keep subversives off the streets, it does not advance understanding of life in the twentieth century. In reality, the change in car stereo technology had two gradients: temporal, with older vehicles more likely to have cassette players, and socio-economic, with expensive cars manufactured during a certain time window being more likely to have a CD player.

The culture of the developed world did change during the period when cassette players were displaced by the CD format. However, both technologies belong to precisely the same culture, albeit one undergoing rapid evolution. As late as 25 years after CD use became common, someone playing CDs in computers and stereos was still perfectly likely to own a vehicle with a cassette player.

This hypothetical example is not churlish – for better or for worse, the sound system in a car is something that most people use for a significant percentage of their waking time. Yet, it is not a legitimate marker of modern culture. It says nothing about the habits or the language of the consumer – it doesn't even indicate which music is likely to be played.

Both systems are soon going to disappear in favour of mp3 format and its successors. Now, that will be a marker of genuine change, for the use of mp3 format requires a home computer and a very different way of recorded music usage.

At the time of writing the author possesses two vehicles, located in different countries. One only has a cassette player. The other has a CD player as well. So much for using material culture to track cultural change.

Returning to our dilemmas, the marker of Indo-European culture is the tumulus burial, otherwise known as a *kurgan*. That structure usually consists of a hole dug in flat terrain, its walls reinforced by logs or stones and covered over with earth, forming a hollow mound. The fact that kurgans are rare in some Indo-European regions (for instance, Northern Europe) is used as evidence against the Kurgan hypothesis.

However, the problem may boil down to simple expediency, such as supply of fuel and the difficulty of digging local soil. Cremation is pointless in the steppe – space is not a problem, but firewood is at a premium. There is, on the other hand, every reason to cremate in densely populated India, where shortage of land and contamination of the water table are major problems, but trees grow aplenty. Proto-Indo-Europeans who arrived into Scandinavia may have simply found it hard to bury their loved ones during winter, when one is most likely to have such need. It is more or less impossible to dig frozen soil without metal tools (that's after clearing the ground of snow and ice). One can see how fires were used to warm the ground before digging (as was done in the Soviet Gulag system by regulation), and cremation would have been a logical evolution of this process. There is no shortage of wood in Northern Europe.

No Proto-Indo-European writings had survived – in all probability because none were written. Indo-European folklore began to be written down a good millennium after the expansion. That will always limit identification of anything we recover from the earth. There is no cultural trait so specifically Indo-European as to provide proof of a link between any given prehistoric culture, identified by distinct archaeological artefacts, and Proto-Indo-Europeans.

But debates about the shapes of ceramic vessels are a lot safer than venturing into the swamp of Indo-European sociology. Gimbutas waded in from the politically correct side, lamenting the horrible misdeeds of her ancestors. Alas, no one has the courage to desist from post-modern value judgement and study the Proto-Indo-European for what he was – a finely honed predator – without mixing political correctness with facts.

This is something of a puzzle to a practitioner of "hard" sciences. No biologist would deny that predators survive by killing prey and tearing it to quivering pieces. No responsible veterinarian would recommend a vegetarian diet for a feline or deny that cats have razor-sharp teeth and claws. No one tries to claim that birds, which cats proudly deposit in front of one's breakfast, have all died of old age.

But archaeology, despite Jonathan Swift's timely warning about Little Endians and Big Endians, remains mired in raging controversies about whether people who buried their deceased in a foetal position were so different from those who laid them out straight.

This is a world away from pointing out that fanatical Americans and fanatical Iranians should concentrate on a common heritage of three millennia, rather than differences that go back a mere generation.

Likewise, only a brave historian would point out that Arabs are risking their entire civilization when they attack the West, although history clearly shows what the West does with such challenges. However, assertions along those lines may have a deleterious effect on one's tenure and mortgage.

Contemporary authorities in Indo-European studies generally stick to safe territory, such as debunking the feminist ravings of Gimbutas. Unfortunately, they are too late to break up the cults she created, and they are too keen to discard, with the feminist bathwater, the factual baby of horsemen from the Pontic steppe. At least Gimbutas had the courage to state the obvious, as depressing as her vision may have been.

Some arguments raised to thwart her are interesting. Alas, the basics of the Kurgan Hypothesis – a violent culture arising from the Pontic steppe and spreading throughout Eurasia – has been tested in full and remains standing.

One alternative hypothesis suggests that the trigger for peaceful Indo-European migration (rather than military expansion) was the collapse of a narrow land barrier that isolated the Black Sea from the Mediterranean, some 3,900 years ago (this figure has recently come under attack from recent evidence, pushing it back to some 7,000 years ago). If the Black Sea was once a freshwater lake that suddenly became salty, there may have been unforeseen circumstances, indeed.

However, today it is jumping with fish (where it is not polluted beyond all hope), and it is hard to imagine anyone starving along its shoreline. Being accessible to the Mediterranean traffic may have caused new grief to the inhabitants of its shore, but it is unlikely that any invader could have come in large numbers via that route during that era, driving the inhabitants of the Pontic region elsewhere.

Regardless of what initiated the Indo-European expansion, one still has to account for the gigantic territory that ended up in the hands of Indo-European language speakers.

Peaceful migration has always created hybrids – bilingual and bicultural subpopulations. Whilst such migrant groups induce some degree of change in the host culture, they do not replace it. Rome did not become Iberian or Egyptian. America did not become German, Italian or Jewish – not even Spanish. Russia, presently the recipient of migrants from all over the former USSR, is unlikely to do more than borrow a few more words from its neighbours, and it is certainly not about to convert to Islam.

On the contrary – history suggests that descendants of migrants assimilate in the host country, and they take great umbrage when their allegiance to it is questioned in any manner. Cultural conversion of the host through peaceful migration is not plentiful in recorded history, and there is no reason to presume that it was otherwise before history began to be recorded.

Some scholars point to the gradual nature of the spread of Indo-European languages and practices as evidence against violent conquest. That objection wouldn't ring true for anyone who ever marched (or even rode) long distances in full kit. Modern-style holocausts were borne on the wings of modern transport. As fast as Proto-Indo-European invaders did their work, they could not cover the entire span of Eurasia in less than a few centuries.

Ancient invaders took time to digest their prey, and when they failed to take such time for digestion, their conquest was short-lived. Nevertheless, a conquest that spread from valley to valley over generations still constitutes a conquest.

The most fallacious objection against Gimbutas' hypothesis rests on the lack of genetic change in Eurasian populations. The genetic make-up of most Europeans (80%, on recent analysis) indicates a continuity with Palaeolithic populations of their native regions.

It is hard to understand why this objection is

even raised. Gimbutas specifically stated that no genetic change took place, the Kurgan people having a cultural, rather than genetic, impact.

To restate that objection more logically, it is hard to imagine how a culture that originated near the Urals had expanded to cover most of the world's largest continent in prehistoric times. It is even more of a strain on credibility to suggest that the said prehistoric culture was so fundamentally different and so dominant, that today its descendants still stand out, whatever latter cultural constructs they wear on top of their Indo-European identity.

It is indeed a strain on common sense – but the recorded history of the past 3,000 years says that it was so. Lightning-fast expansion by Indo-Europeans that annihilated a large range of native cultures is a fact, which we are still living today.

Greeks, Romans, Spaniards, Britons and Russians all came in minuscule numbers to new lands, trounced the natives on the battlefield, changed the landscape to their liking and then blended into the native population within a few generations – but the changes in the local culture remained.

Alas, most objections against the Kurgan Hypothesis are little more scientific than Gimbutas' utopian visions about matriarchal "Old Europe". Alas, most of these objections are driven by an unscientific motive – a desire to refute one monstrous fact – that "we" are inheritors of the world's most violent culture.

Attempts to fit facts into a view always lead to the dreary Valhalla of pseudo-science, in which the spirits of Mead and Gimbutas dine alongside ideologues of white supremacy. It cannot be much of a dinner party.

One can understand the distaste of some professionals; it is too easy to turn the anthropology of Indo-European expansion into a comic book. The first instalment was about Gimbutas' bloodthirsty male berserkers. They club to death, a la Canadian seal hunt, the still-lactating matriarchs of "Old Europe", and the world turns bad.

The next learned comic book presents an image of misunderstood, peace-loving Aryans who flee some kind of ecological catastrophe in the Pontic region. Apparently, goes that story, the refugees were resettled by such gracious hosts that the latter decided to throw away their language and culture in favour of their unfortunate guests, presumably out of sheer sympathy.

Modern reality offers many examples of cultural clashes as a result of migration. Sometimes one group of migrants manages to displace another without bloodshed, such as Hispanics transforming the English-speaking Southern

USA – or Pacific and Asian immigrants changing the face of Australia and New Zealand.

However, the overall theme seems to be that nobody gives up their identity voluntarily. Even the most disempowered of natives, such as the Pygmies of Southern Africa or Australian Aborigines, put up a fight when someone tries to pull their ethnic identity from under their feet.

Yes, the history of Indo-Europeans is replete with appalling bloodshed. Worst still, we will never know what opportunities were lost through annihilation of vibrant cultures that made the mistake of competing with Indo-Europeans militarily or just getting in the way – from the inventors of the alphabet and seafaring, the Carthaginians, to the Australian Aborigines, whose unique bush culture offers fascinating insights into human development, is disappearing faster than anyone can document it.

The truth about Indo-Europeans is not politically correct. They killed their opponents and survived long enough to see others collapse. That is how produced the largest sphere of influence of any other cultural grouping on Earth.

How we deal with these historic facts is up to us. What is not up to anyone is to distort them.

"Indo-Europeans do not always win"

So says J P Mallory, in an evident and understandable attempt to side-step the Gimbutas model.

Quite so, not always. However, in all significant instances of Indo-Europeans losing to other cultures, the invader had been seduced and assimilated into Indo-European culture.

The bottom line is that the world is an Indo-European village – because Indo-Europeans cajoled, subjugated and sliced to ribbons anyone who got in the way. Indo-Europeans were not the only ones to engage in such behaviour, but their success proved the most consistent in the long run.

It is true that some nations adopted Indo-European customs, if not languages, voluntarily. Also, many former colonies of Indo-Europeans had voluntarily retained crucial aspects of Indo-European culture after their masters left. But recorded history is quite conclusive – the favourite method of Indo-European spread is violent domination.

There are few instances of complete Indo-European roll-back – Indo-European culture seldom surrenders ground. In recent colonial times "going native" was regarded as a form of dropping out of respectable society, an act of unsound and probably unwell individuals – not, under any circumstances, a social trend, even when a conquered culture offered sophistication and a lengthy pedigree of its own.

Most of the former colonies of Europe have been independent for more than three generations. In some cases, such as in Africa, there is no longer a native Caucasian population. But there is no instance of any African country returning to its pre-colonization culture. For what they are worth, the institutions of these countries are Indo-European.

Non-Indo-European nations of Asia and Africa have copied so many aspects of European lifestyle that their lifestyle is little different from their compatriots who emigrated to Western countries.

The Huns, who nearly subjugated Europe in a very similar manner to the Mongols, simply came and went. We do not even know who they were, ethnically or racially. If they were Asiatic, they left no genetic legacy in Europe. Unlike Mongols they suffered military setbacks at the hands of Europeans who stemmed the Hun invasion, and lack of strong national ethos did the rest – the Huns simply disappeared as a nation.

The Mongols were a true non-Indo-European

challenge to the survival of Indo-Europeans – they devastated Russia, Central Europe, the Middle East and Asia Minor. They got as far as Hungary in the west and India in the east, and if they were so inclined, they could have snuffed out all descendants of Proto-Indo-Europeans.

Having come from the region still described by the borders of modern Mongolia, they partially adopted the administrative and decorative aspects of Chines culture after taking China. The Mongols later converted, some to Christianity and others to Islam. Neither conversion made much difference to their politics, with subsequent targets being Muslims and Christians in equal measure.

But herein lies the difference – Mongols were not cultural hegemonists. In Russia, which they ruled for three hundred years, they made not the slightest effort to change either culture or religion of their subjects. Only a few Mongolian words had entered Russian language because the victor had to be communicated with on his terms.

But Mongols did not at all mind that Russians remained true to Slavonic and Christian traditions. Far from it, the Golden Horde used Russian nobility and the apparatus of the Russian Orthodox Church to do most of the dirty work. Even as the top echelons of the Golden Horde became ardent Muslims, they continued to show total indifference to the religious preferences of their vassals.

Largely, it is this tolerant attitude that caused Mongols to leave such a small cultural legacy. Mongolian customs and language now matter only to the population of Mongolia and a few small enclaves in China and Russia. Today ethnic Mongols are a tiny population largely confined to their homeland, whose alphabet and other modern institutions are adapted, ironically, from Russia.

It is true that a descendant of Mongol rulers carried Islam to southern Asia, establishing the Mogul dynasty in India. But that was done by Iranian nobles of vague Mongolian descent, whose ancestors resided in Islamic Persia for some four generations prior to coming south. After Arabs and Turks Mongols became the last of those who invaded Iran as nomads, but left a few generations later, Iranian to the bone.

There are a few instances of genuine erasure of Indo-European culture. In most cases, however, Indo-European were displaced genetically (in simple words, killed off or ran away). One has to scrape the barrel for places where a surviving Indo-European population accepted the culture of invader.

The Tarim Basin is located on the southern edge of the Gobi Desert in north-western China. It was once home to the Indo-European Tocharians, who vanished in a rare example of wholesale cultural conversion. Today the native culture and language are Uighur (Turkic). There appears to be no demonstrable remnant of Indo-European religion, social structure or language, which were believed to have become extinct at the beginning of first millennium AD.

Tocharian culture is relatively well documented because of their interactions with the neighbouring Buddhist monasteries. We even know remarkable details about their lifestyle, thanks to a collection of mummified remains in a perfect state of preservation, going back to 2000 BC.

From these sources it is known that Tocharians spoke and wrote an Indo-European language. Their artefacts as well as language suggest a kinship to the Celts of Western Europe. The genetic analysis of the mummies also points to a Western European lineage. They appear to have used horse wagons with wheels nearly identical to those found in the contemporary Pontic region, and they were expert metal workers and weavers.

Their burial practices will be familiar enough to the reader of these pages – earth mounds with the burial crypt shored up with logs – and human sacrifices. One Tarim mummy is of a young woman with long blond hair, whose arms were mutilated and eyes gouged out. A toddler aged around twelve months appears to have been buried alive.

Even allowing for a change of climate, Tocharians must have led a hard life in a barely arable land. The Tarim lake is believed to have dried up around the beginning of the first millennium, and it believed that Tocharians were conquered by Chinese, then by Turkic Uighurs, who were themselves forcibly joined to China in the Middle Ages.

Today the region is inhabited by mainly Muslim Uighurs, many of whom exhibit a mix of Caucasoid and Asiatic characteristics. This is evidence that many Tocharians had survived the conquest.

It can be said, therefore, that the roll-back of Indo-European culture was complete in the area of the Tarim Basin: there was no wholesale killing of the Indo-European population, but its survivors lost all connection with their Indo-European past. It is possible that Uighurs overran the remnant of the Tocharians and enslaved them – which still kept them in the gene pool but without opportunity to practise their culture. This is far more likely than a scenario where a population is pressured into changing cultures by a conquering elite.

Turkic migrations have displaced, rather than converted, the Iranian population of Central Asia.

Some of their descendants retained the ethos, lifestyle and language of their ancestors (Kazakh and Kyrgyz people even have sovereign states). Other Turkic speakers underwent subsequent conversion to Iranian culture in the Middle Ages (Tajiks, Azeris and the Afghan Khazars).

Norse population in Greenland has experienced a complete roll-back, as a result of an opposite climatic change. The Norse were replaced by Inuit people, whose technology was better adapted to the cold – even if this was not a case of Norsemen being conquered and forced to speak another language (as one understands the present evidence, the Norse simply left, clashes with the Inuit hunters being only one of the incentives to do so). The fairest accusation that can be levied against the Norse is that they failed to adapt, even though they were perfectly capable of switching their diet to seafood and still maintaining valuable trade in whale products with Europe.

Ugro-Finnic-speaking people who migrated out of the Ural homeland west and north-west had left population pockets all along these routes. The outer extreme of that migration appears to have been the Baltic shore, where today they reside in nations of Estonia and Finland. The rest live as small minorities embedded in the Russian hinterland, their culture and first language being Russian. They had no choice but to adopt many

European institutions, but they nevertheless remain distinct from the Indo-Europeans who dominated them for centuries.

But Proto-Ugro-Finnic migration is now believed to pre-date the Indo-European expansion, and according to the latest view, the modern Ugro-Finnic speakers in the Baltic region, Russia and Scandinavia are survivors, not subsequent invaders.

On the other hand, a separate population of Ugro-Finnic speakers, known as Magyars, forced their way into the Hungarian plain some time after the collapse of Roman rule. This region was once firmly Indo-European territory, but left devastated after the Huns. Arriving a few centuries on, the Magyars, possibly from Central Asia, brought their language and culture, both of which they successfully forced on the local Indo-European population. Like Finns, post-Magyar Hungarians had no choice but copy many habits of surrounding Indo-Europeans, but theirs is the largest population in Europe that does not speak an Indo-European language.

Turkish conquest of the Greek-speaking Asia Minor has resulted in a linguistic conversion – but by the time that conquest was complete, the nomadic Turkic culture of the ruling elite was but a memory. Turkish has replaced original languages in a relatively small proportion of the former Turkish empire, but failed to do so elsewhere – in the Balkan region, Greece, Armenia and Kurdistan. Subsequently, Turkey lost a large slice of Turkic-speaking territory in the Pontic region, which today is firmly in Slavonic hands. Turks were also expelled from the territories they briefly conquered in Central Europe, leaving no significant legacy.

Despite its official religion and language, Ottoman Turkey was as much a part of the European world as any contemporary nation of Europe. There was an extensive trade, along with which came exchange of customs and technology. The main divide was political – consequent upon the Turkish campaigns against Europeans – and, to a lesser extent, Islam, although Turks never ran their campaigns under the banner of holy wars. During most of the Ottoman era Europeans regarded Christian Russians with possibly greater hostility – and even sided with Turkey against Russia in Crimea. There was an extensive cultural exchange between Turkey and Europe.

The original Turks came from Central Asia, but then settled in Iran, whose culture they adopted in full and with whose population they freely intermarried. Turkey subsequently received fresh batches of Turkic migrants, who found a ready acceptance in a triumphant army, whose language they still understood without coaching.

By the time they made their way over the

massive walls of Constantinople, the beating heart of Indo-European culture in the East, the Turks were Indo-European in all but name. Many Turkish sultans were tall Caucasians, the original Asiatic appearance of Turkic tribesmen and their nomadic culture being some twenty generations distant.

Much of the administrative corps of the Turkish empire was recruited from Serbian and Croatian regions. The elite Turkish troops were Janissaries, modelled on the Egyptian Mamelukes. These were also former boy slaves, predominantly captured in the Balkans. Eastern Europeans contributed heavily to the rest of the Turkish army: Ottomans offered provinces an option of providing men for military service instead of paying tax.

Modern Turkish population has a greater percentage of Central Asian gene markers than surrounding Caucasian populations. But in the main, modern Turks are largely descendants of Byzantine Indo-Europeans, undisputed masters of Asia Minor since at least sixth century BC.

Today Turkey's Indo-European population (who for nearly ten centuries spoke Greek) speaks a Turkic language and subscribes to an Arab religion. But Islam still left Turks with an Indo-European culture and mass psychology. That simple fact was lost on those who battled the Turkish Empire, much to their detriment.

Today, much as ever, the backbone of Turkish society is a large, well-disciplined army, which behaves as a state within a state. It serves as a powerful counterweight to the excesses of civilian politics, an economic flywheel and a stabilizing social institution. Unlike many such armies, it has a long tradition of battle-worthiness, enjoying a healthy respect of its recent opponents.

No one would imagine Turkey as anything other than a European nation, were its population predominantly Christian – yet both Christianity and Islam are foreign, latter and more superficial social layers that cloak older and more fundamental traits of social character.

In the centuries when most conversations in Europe revolved around the conflict with Turkey, Turks were portrayed as cruel and barbarous occupiers of formerly Christian lands. Alas, this another case of the Carthage syndrome: Europeans of the time committed equally unspeakable horrors on their own soil, let alone against Christian neighbours. In the Holy Land, where Ottomans did not encounter ongoing opposition, their rule marked the most peaceful and humane era in the bloody history of the region.

As a result the Turks (who know who they are) feel bewilderment at the steadfast refusal to let them join Europe, despite a solid century of cooperation with the West, often to Turkey's detriment.

Turning to other examples of Indo-European roll-back, many former colonies of European nations are busy erasing the legacy of occupation – as much as such erasure may be meaningful in the world that speaks English and dines at MacDonald's.

Southern Africa and Rhodesia may be viewed as two nations occupied by Indo-Europeans who did not give up control of their dominions willingly, as opposed to the voluntary departure of other colonial powers. Both capitulated to native guerrillas aided by Marxist powers, and both were cajoled into surrender by Western powers, who betrayed Southern Africa in the interest of political expediency. It cannot be seriously argued that either Rhodesia or South Africa could ever have been toppled by direct military assault from any local opponent.

The winners of that mainly political struggle were African tribesmen, who are not proposing a wholesale return to the semi-nomadic Stone Age culture of their ancestors – but, strictly speaking, that too is a roll-back for Indo-Europeans.

The remaining challenger

Today the sole remaining challenge to the global Indo-European supremacy comes from the Islamic world. This loose term defines an umbrella grouping of various cultures, many of whom are Indo-European. Conversion to Islam makes Afghans, Pakistanis and Bosnians no more Arab than conversion of Germans and Russians to Christianity makes them Jewish. Within the Islamic grouping Malayans and Indonesians have much in common with each other and little in common with Arabs, Albanians or Chechens.

Likewise, nations like Egypt, Jordan and Turkey are firmly on the western side. It is not strictly possible, therefore, to regard the conflict between Islam and the West as Indo-Europeans versus non-Indo-Europeans.

Islamic nations have all had extensive contacts with Indo-Europeans at many points in their history. As soon as they galloped out of Arab Peninsula, the Arabs became aware that they faced an uphill cultural battle. They were desert nomads who conquered Mesopotamians, Egyptians, Iranians and Romans. In the span of a few generations Arabs crossed the Pyrenees, landed on the Atlantic coast of Africa and marched into Hindu Kush – homelands of ancient and sophisticated civilizations. Apart from the new religion and a few loan words from the invaders' language, the transfer of culture could only go one way.

Only a century later we witness the splendour of Baghdad and Moorish Spain, the magnificence of their architecture, a bubbling torrent of scientific and technological advances, a humane and rational approach to government and an intrepid exploration in trade, all successes worthy of magnificent Arab poetry.

The ingredients of that success did not come from the aboriginal culture of Arab Peninsula, which was barely Iron Age at the time of Mohammed. Most of what is known as Islamic civilization came from Iran, and the rest came from Byzantine Greeks, Semites and Copts who comprised the population of pre-Islamic Middle East. The Arab contribution to that thriving culture lay in the immediate uptake of useful ideas encountered along the way.

As an intellectual exercise, one could consider what would become of Islamic civilization if instead of taking the Middle East and Central Asia, conveniently bled white by the ongoing conflict between Indo-Europeans, the Arabs went on to conquer sub-Saharan Africa instead.
Arabs were always a small minority in the Islamic world; their ancestral tribes were confined to the region that starts in the south of

modern Israel and extends through the Arabian peninsula. Many other ethnicities now speak Arabic as their first language: modern Egyptians, Lybians, Tunisians and Moroccans are not Arabs, and neither are Lebanese, Syrians or Iraqis. These are native populations of their respective regions – Berbers, Egyptian Copts, Syrians, Babylonians and Assyrians. Even so, the speakers of Arabic and practitioners of Arab culture are a relatively small minority amongst Muslims.

Islamic world has wrestled with the West for fourteen centuries, and at times the West came close to losing. Even assuming that it has seen the apogee of its success, it has to be said that Islam has succeeded, like no other challenger to the Indo-European world, in splitting it into Muslims and others.

For instance, Islam was adopted in Albania and Bosnia, which obfuscated the essential Indo-European identity of the respective populations (Christianity not being a part of that essential identity), to the point where genetically identical Serbs and Bosniaks consider themselves mortal enemies. Descendants of Zoroastrians and Buddhists, the citizens of Afghanistan and Pakistan do not remember their pre-Islamic past – but they still fight like Indo-Europeans. Western troops, adorned with crisp uniforms and cologne, are sent into the oldest flashpoints in Eurasia because their generals fail to realize this simple fact.

The divide between Islam and non-Islam is what sets one Indian against another, and it is the same divide that sets Americans and Europeans against Iranians. Islam remains the shibboleth of the Caucasus, despite most of its adult inhabitants being brought up in the strict atheism of the Soviet era. The first rebel leader of the Chechens rose to the rank of general in the Soviet Air Force, being thoroughly and repeatedly vetted against any religious affiliations. If a practising Muslim, he would never have made the officer academy.

It can be argued that Indo-Europeans enjoy a stranglehold on military supremacy in the Islamic world, much as their Christian cousins do elsewhere. Tensions between the West and non-Indo-European Muslims, such as Malays and Indonesians, certainly exist, but their leadership is all too aware of lacking the military muscle to make good on such sentiments.

Within three centuries of the rise of Islam, Indo-Europeans have wrested control of the Muslim world from the Arabs. The first effective blow against the Crusader Kingdom was struck by Salah-Ad-Din, a Kurdish native of Iran. He did not succeed in expelling the Crusaders – that honour fell to Baybars, the sultan of the Mamelukes – another interesting piece in the

Indo-European mosaic.

Successors to the Kurdish dynasty of which Salah-Ad-Din was the most illustrious leader, the Mamelukes were former slaves, purchased as boys from Eastern and Southern Europe and brought to Egypt to join its army. Some Mamelukes must have been Turkic, but evidence suggests that most were not. Mamelukes were kidnapped or captured in wars rather than bred from existing slaves.

They rapidly evolved into a ruling warrior class, which remained entirely aloof from Egyptian society: the Mamelukes took native wives but raised boys in isolation from native culture. It can be said that Egypt became a country in the service of a foreign army.

The Mameluke psyche consisted of devotion to war and total contempt for life – theirs and everybody else's. It is not difficult to trace the origin of that heritage.

Today most wars fought by Islam feature Indo-Europeans: Pakistanis, Iranians, Afghans, Chechens, Bosniaks and Albanians. After a little reflection, this makes sense.

Islam is a military creed – an ersatz militaristic culture. It deliberately constructs the military-industrial-cultural complex that Indo-European cultures maintain subliminally, by tradition. The result is a potent mix indeed, especially when

Indo-Europeans hardened by fourteen centuries of Islam face Indo-Europeans softened by two centuries of domestic safety and material self-indulgence.

Even Indo-Europeans such as Russians, whose living conditions and attitudes to human life match those of Muslim opponents, are finding that it takes more than ruthlessness and brutality to defeat the likes of Afghans and Chechens. The Russian army's tactics in both conflicts were reasonably sound – but progress slowed to a crawl because both sides shared the same mentality. Neither party was easily demoralized with firepower or shocked with civilian atrocities.

So very well – Indo-Europeans do not always win, but they lose very infrequently. Also, one ventures to say, the present state of the world should not be mistaken for the final outcome of the conflict between Islam and the West. It is not as if Indo-European predators are extinct – Russia, if none other, is entirely capable of realizing its centuries-long ambition of flying its flags over the source of its culture, Constantinople, presently known as Istanbul.

The fact that Indo-Europeans had lost some of their gains does not disprove the existence or the effectiveness of their militaristic culture. In fact, there is no reason why any aggressor should always win – that would be unnatural. Rome, that most vicious of predators, had lost battles and campaigns on a frequent basis, but no one would deny its predatory nature on the basis of such failure.

Even overwhelming firepower is no guarantee of unending success: a rifle company can be successfully attacked with spears and stones. The towering might of a modern army can be worn down by a determined guerilla force armed with outdated weapons. This is especially so today, when sophisticated military technology is available to anyone with dollars, and a plane worth half a billion dollars can be brought down with a missile worth a few thousand.

It is no miracle that Huns and Mongols produced hordes that rode down Indo-European opponents, just as the latter rode down their enemies in prehistory. Mongols and Huns were trained from childhood to ride and shoot from the saddle, and a disciplined body of such warriors would even endanger a modern army, Indo-European or not.

Weapons and tactics are easily copied – in the long run, what matters most is motivation.

Urheimat

The obsession with the exact origin of Proto-Indo-European culture is easy to understand – it is a game that many nations play for high stakes, considering the power of nationalism in the last two centuries.

Since Napoleon, Europeans have been grouped into arbitrary ethnic conglomerates, and chauvinistic sentiment that glued such entities became a major driver of global politics.

Pinning down the origin of Indo-Europeans in a convincing manner would be worth more than a nuclear arsenal in the currency of national prestige. It is not surprising that nations from Norway to India vie for that claim.

Known by its German term Urheimat, or land of origin, that hypothetical and largely mythical area has been broadly agreed to lie where Gimbutas placed it – somewhere to the north of the land bridge between Black and Caspian Seas.

On the balance of solid archaeological facts along with much circumstantial evidence, this does look like a likely jump-off point for Indo-European conquest of Eurasia. If one draws all intersecting lines of linguistic and technological trends, they have a stubborn tendency of intersecting in a relatively small region between the Russian cities of Voronezh and Saratov.

There are a number of less credible alternatives, which the rest of this chapter will examine briefly, for completeness.

There is a school of militant Hindus called Hindutva, who proposed a "from India" model of Aryan migration. According to this model, supported by little physical evidence, India never suffered an Aryan invasion (or, as modern scholarship prefers to suggest, a gradual migration from modern Afghanistan into the subcontinent). The adherents of that school cite disjointed archaeological facts, for most of which one can cite an alternative explanation.

There is no physical reason why Indo-Europeans could not have come from Northern India (although Aryan myths and much else tends to contradict this), migrated north to the steppe at the base of the Urals in small numbers, then flourished in that new homeland and commenced the Eurasian expansion from the Pontic region, finding themselves back in India centuries later.

But tracing these movements is beyond the plausible limits of scientific method. Today it only serves to distract from more important issues.

The dating of finds related to the Aryan migration into India reflects its spread over many generations, during which pre-Indo-European population co-existed with the new arrivals. Likewise, the modern Rig Veda, used as much of the source of this material, was added to as late as 900 BC, which makes it impossible to determine whether its earliest texts, possibly composed as early as 1700 BC, pre-date the other known references to Indo-Europeans outside of India.

The archaeological facts are plain – no Indian artefacts, related to Indo-European culture, pre-date those of the Hittites. There are also older Babylonian records that refer to the Indo-European gods of the Hurrians (possibly as early as 1500BC). It is therefore unlikely that Proto-Indo-Europeans originated in India.

According to a model based on estimated rates of language drift over time and distance, (which is not universally recognized), Proto-Indo-Europeans came from Northern Anatolia. Some facts, such as the chronology of horse remains in India, indicate that Aryans may have originated there and came north before spreading to a vast area we see now.

The proposed formulae used by adherents of the drift model would work well for a new gene spreading through a pond full of amoebae, but cultures do not diffuse according to a formula. One subpopulation may gallop to overtake its close relatives, and their language "gradient" over distance will not obey simple mathematical models. This can occur for totally random local reasons, such as technological advances, advantages of terrain or unusually effective leaders.

One can cite numerous examples: English loan words now abound in modern European languages. Modern Russians, for instance, have not even bothered with trying to use native words for "business", "manager" or even "appointment". English-sourced technical terms like "file" and "hacker" abound in every modern language. This cannot be used as evidence of the British conquering Russia or living there in significant numbers.

In the past linguistic influence was less likely to occur without the actual speakers moving to a new domain in numbers – but they could have done so as nomads or traders – and even exiles or slaves. During the recorded history of Anatolia there were dozens of such shifts, and nothing can be assumed about its prehistory either.

By definition, prehistory is a period that pre-dates records, either written or as information handed down through generations. Prehistoric cultures, especially nomadic, originated in broad areas and underwent gradual maturation. Where prehistoric cultures communicated, their traits formed a continuum from which individualized nationalities would gradually emerge.

To illustrate the problem, we still can't pinpoint the homeland of Huns. The most precise and factual answer is "North-West China", but that covers a meaninglessly large expanse. This is despite the fact that Huns traversed the territories of three highly literate civilizations – Chinese, Iranian and Roman – and did so relatively recently.

Thankfully, no one seems to dispute that the Hun movement is a solid historic fact, despite a negligible archaeological record to testify to the Huns' existence. Even though they nearly overran Europe, there are few European records that even make mention of the Huns. The facts are so sketchy that we don't even know what they looked like (the most common Roman description being "hideous"). It is not even known whether Huns were Asiatic or Caucasian.

This is because Proto-Huns were not builders of fortresses, temples or roads. They were nomadic horsemen who ranged all over a vast, featureless region, on which they seldom left little more than rubbish heaps. At some stage their national characteristics began to take a distinct shape, probably with increasing coalescence, under the banner of one chieftain after another.

The geographic centre of Proto-Hun territory probably shifted around the Eurasian steppe, covering millions of square miles in the course of that evolution. As they moved west, they would have acquired many allies and companions – their customs and appearance being, therefore, amorphous and hard to describe by the time they reached the eyes of literate Romans.

Preliterate nomads leave only burials, which sometimes are found intact. More often the graves are either ravaged or simply lost. In moist earth human remains can disappear after a few years – contrary to popular belief, bones will be broken down if there is enough bacterial activity.

When nomads practise cremation, they leave few remains that allow meaningful study. The only archaeological record will be confined to totally accidental preservation of "strays" who die in unusual places or circumstances, becoming mummified in deserts, tanned in bogs, snap-freezing in permafrost or glaciers. Being larger and more compacted, mass graves provide a dismal exception – yet nomads seldom exert themselves to dig them, preferring to simply pack their belongings and move away from a contaminated site. Animals then consume and scatter all surface remains of a massacre.

Even where they exist – and this is a major problem with reconstruction of pre-history – grave goods can only say so much. For a true feel of an ancient culture one needs a record, oral or written, to supplement what can be gleaned from archaeological data.

The question of a Hun origin is therefore invalid a priori.

Likewise, we could search for the origin of modern Germans or Russians. But nominating such an origin would be most unlikely to cast a new light on towering cultures that grew from a cluster of muddy villages. It would not deepen one's understanding of Goethe or Dostoevsky.

Consider another nomadic nation, whose history is exquisitely documented and cherished by its descendants. We have but a vague idea about the origin of the Hebrews, first mentioned in Egyptian (and other) sources as brigands and mercenaries named *Hapiru* – meaning "across the river".

Which river, and does it even flow today? The story of Abraham (which is entirely beyond any possible proof or disproof) suggests that *Hapiru* came from somewhere in Mesopotamia. Other contenders are Egypt and Idumea (the south of modern Jordan).

An Egyptian stele, cut around 1200 BC, mentions Israel by name for the first time. From that inscription it appears to be a nation of military substance. Its location is presumed to be close to Egypt, but this is not discernible from the text.

It is possible that one day someone will unearth a Sumerian text unequivocally referring to

Abraham's departure. That may sway a few of those who consider the Bible inaccurate. Jewish nationalists would make a meal of that information.

But nothing else would change. Given the subsequent changes in genes, places, languages and beliefs, is it likely that knowing the precise origin of the Jews would shed brighter light on the subsequent development of Jewish culture? No.

Likewise, one sees little profit in trying to pinpoint Urheimat to a specific district of modern Turkey, Russia or Ukraine.

Let us turn from Urheimat and focus on the big picture. Three quarters of the world's population speak an Indo-European language. There are virtually no modern people whose culture has not been influenced by the Indo-European expansion.

The Volga is one of the largest river systems in the world. Its delta is two miles wide, making it difficult to see one shore from another.

Its origins lie some 2,500 miles away in the Valdai Hills near Moscow. It is possible to sail up that giant waterway, then navigate a smaller river in the Valdai, finally running aground in a forest brook. One could even go further, walking upstream to the place where spring water comes from the redolent moss, destined to join thousands of other such sources as the mighty Volga.

One can allege that a particular forest spring is the origin of the river. But that would be entirely artificial. A study of that spring would say nothing about the river flowing across thousands of kilometres of varying landscapes. None of the spectacular species of large fish species live in the delta are present in a Valdai brook. The wide and varied chemistry of the lower Volga, so polluted "that a film dropped into it is likely to develop", is entirely absent upstream.

The competition for Urheimat is an equally superfluous distraction from the study of the Indo-European phenomenon.

The first critic of the Kurgan role model

The social dynamics of Indo-European culture are vastly more important than its precise ancestral origin. Identification of these dynamics immediately clarifies much of what one observes in the world today, how it came to be and what, if anything, we can do about it – problems that Zarathushtra visualized with remarkable clarity.

Thinkers of his calibre do not come along often, and his appearance around 1700 BC was no accident. Indo-European culture was at a crossroads – the destructive power of its military-industrial juggernaut has become a major limitation on the quality of life and further progress.

Introduction of the chariot intensified carnage and exacerbated the distinction between predators and prey. The damage done by a military-industrial complex devoid of an ethical purpose was equally obvious to any thoughtful observer. That horror had to be brought under control, lest it caused society to self-destruct.

There was an urgent need to define the ethical bounds of violence. This was doubly so because most of that violence did not occur in the context of a protracted war. In Zarathushtra's time everyone doubled as a warrior. Raids and skirmishes were ceaseless and shapeless in social or ethnic terms.

Even today civilized society takes a lot of trouble to prevent former (and present) members of its armed forces from turning their martial skills to crime. This is never entirely successful, despite the fact that trained combatants are a small percentage of most modern populations, and the weapons they are trained to use are difficult to obtain in civilian life.

In post-Communist Russia neither of these circumstances applied, and much of the catastrophic crime that swept Russia in the subsequent decade was perpetrated by ex-military thugs, who retained their weapons after demobilization.

Of greater concern are warriors trained in infiltration of civilian structures for espionage or sabotage. Their activities are much harder to regulate after they return to civilian society. In Russia such people became no mere criminals but official government, whose thuggery quickly eclipsed the misdeeds of ex-soldier privateers.

In the time of Zarathushtra every able-bodied male owned weapons and practised using them to the best of ability. The "lifestyle", to use a politically correct term for daily struggle, meant that combatants were usually at the peak of their physical fitness (unlike modern soldiers, who, for some reason, are allowed to squander themselves on smoking and drinking). That was just as well, as combat could take place with little notice.

Although expertise in violence was ubiquitous, by Zarathushtra's time professional fighters (including bandits) already carried the day over farmers:

The Wise God, the Knowing One, spoke lovingly: So you do not know any lord or leader who acts in righteousness?

(Gathas: xi)

Priests and princes yoke people by force to destroy life with their evil actions.

(Gathas: xi)

Have you control and power, o Mazda of Right and Good Thought, to do as I beg of you, to protect your poor man? We have renounced the marauding gangs, demons and men.

(Gathas: vi)

Before Zarathushtra came forward with the concept of universal morality, no one had a sense of social cohesion outside their immediate clan. Even neighbouring clans were regarded as competitors in the never-ending battle for scarce resources, and elimination of such competition was seen as desirable when the opportunity arose.

Only a universal moral code could stop a man from clouting an outsider over the head to take what didn't belong to him. Allegiance to such a code goes well beyond fearing the consequences of wrong-doing.

Murder is not wrong because the murderer can attract the wrath of Jehovah or become hunted by the relatives of his victim. Calling it wrong is a recognition that it is a practice that doesn't scale – if serious crimes like murder are practised widely, society cannot advance beyond a certain primitive level. Living standards and population size cannot rise above a certain stage of development.

This does not just apply to humans. Unless it is averse to killing its own, a species can only exist as a sparse population of isolated individuals (as, for instance, most snakes), and a relatively small change in environmental circumstances can lead to its extinction, locally or globally (as is happening to many snake species today).

The emergence of a warrior caste made the problem all the more acute. Operating in the early stage of Indo-European social stratification, Zarathushtra was still addressing the amateurs and the hobbyists rather than hereditary warriors, urging them to think of themselves as defenders of righteous causes, rather than glamorous predators.

In times when Indo-European societies could afford to rest on their laurels, they spawned many moral campaigns that attempted to rein in the violent aspects of Indo-European culture. The collective result, otherwise known as political correctness, is composed of the remains of many attempts at "harm minimization" with ethical constructs such as Christian pacifism, Marxist (pseudo) equality or influential Neo-Pagan cults, such as the Wicca movement.

Zarathushtra's model was the first, and, one may contend, the most effective. One possible reason for that success is that it came from an Indo-European who specifically tailored his model to address the fundamental flaw of Indo-European society.

The second possible reason is that in shaping his creed, Zarathushtra made no detours to please existing powers. True to his own moral system, he had the courage to tread across them.

How could false gods be good governors? I ask this because those who act out of lust, with which the mumbling priests have delivered the world to anger, and the princes, in their stubbornness, have forced it to weep, and do not reward it with righteousness in order to encourage a settled life.

(Gathas: ix)

Zarathushtra made a quantum cultural leap when he elevated productivity (what we today call utilitarianism) and its sister, innovation, as the greatest forms of human endeavour. In contrast, witness the Indian Mahabarata or Homer's Iliad. The works of Early Indo-Europeans portray destruction, conquest and slaughter as worthy tasks of heroes and demigods – a brigand ethic, which regards all life-sustaining activities with contempt.

To understand what Zarathushtra took on, consider the Iliad – an epic glorifying the destruction of a major population centre, if not an entire civilization, at enormous expense, effort and toll.

No plunder of Troy could have made good on the costs of the expedition and a lengthy siege, supplied from across the sea at such an early stage of technological development. That Clockwork-Orange-style hoodlum picnic was frightening enough at a time of swords and arrows. Now imagine it in the age of computers, submarines and ballistic missiles.

As in the time of Zarathushtra, the modern world lacks observers brave enough to gaze into the mirror. But not entirely.

It was with some surprise that I once heard Tony Blair, the British Prime Minister at the time of writing. He commented, quite matter-of-factly, on the origin of English soccer hooliganism. He related it to the fact that the present generation of young Englishmen is the third not to go to a major war.

That was a very insightful observation, which goes to the core of many Indo-European dilemmas. It is unfortunate that such moments of clarity are few and far between.

A statuette found at Arkaim, dubbed "The Thinker"

Zoroastrianism was the second "upgrade" of Indo-European religion to survive to modern day. We are privileged to have a fairly precise idea of what the original religion of Indo-Europeans looked like, for Hinduism is very much with us and, whilst it undoubtedly changed over four millennia, its ancient sacred texts are well preserved and convey a good idea of what its practitioners had to say at least 3,500 years ago.

Whilst Hinduism is sneered at by followers of more "sophisticated" religions, it is the only polytheistic religion outside, perhaps, Japan's Shintoism, that survives and thrives in an industrialized society. The old religion of Indo-Europeans was not designed as a moral system, but Hinduism had plenty of time to make up for this, being, possibly, the world's oldest living religion.

Hinduism is regarded as a mainstream representative of Indo-European religions that inherited many characteristics of the original Proto-Indo-European religion from which they all derived.

Daeus Phater ("father god") appears to be common to all known representatives of early Indo-European pantheon: for instance, Greek Zeus, Latin Jupiter, proto-Hindu Dyaus,

Lithuanian Dievas, Gaelic Dispatr, Germanic Tiyus or Slavonic Diy. The father god is generally considered supreme and the honorary elder in the pantheon.

There is a less well emphasized mother goddess, a counterpart to the stern, ruthless and occasionally sadistic father god, represented by the Greek Demeter ("the mother") or the Latvian Zemes Mate and the Slavonic Mata Zemlje (literally, "mother of earth").

There is a god of thunder and war – Perun amongst the Slavs, Perkunos to the Balts, Fjorgyn (Thor) to Scandinavians, Taran to the Celts and Tarjun to the Hittites.

Other gods enjoy variable emphasis, such as the Sanskrit god of the underworld, Varuna, or the Greek Aphrodite.

The pantheon of Indo-Europeans as they evolved and migrated clearly exhibited an amorphous flexibility, with gods competing for contemporaneous relevance. Some gods changed their job descriptions, and others found their positions merged or made redundant. For instance, the original father god of the Greeks was Chronos, the father (and devourer) of all other gods, against whom Zeus successfully rebelled. The Greek Poseidon was lumbered with the underworld (including tectonic activity), which may seem a somewhat illogical combination of jobs, especially for a maritime nation. Likewise, gods could be displaced by a foreign equivalent – for instance, the Greek Helios was eclipsed by Apollo, a migrant from adjacent Anatolia.

A Russian scholar Alexander Fantalov even proposed a broad classification with five categories of Indo-European deities. He postulated that these represented the five archetypical gods of proto-Indo-Europeans: He suggested the god of the sky, the god of thunder, the god of the underworld, a god hero (such as Hercules) and a single female goddess, along the lines of Demeter.

There are also common elements in Indo-European mythology, such as the great tree of the world (Ygdrasil of the Norse and the Banyan tree of the Hindu). It became a less abstract symbol amongst other Indo-Europeans, such as the oak tree of the Slavonics and the Germanics, or a hazel tree amongst the Celts.

Another common element is a story of a hero god battling and slaying a serpent. Thor did away with Jormungandr, and Apollo did the same with the Python. Hercules attended to the Hydra, and Indra killed Virytra. St George even manages to ride into the Christian pantheon through the same achievement. With obvious symbolism, this myth is not restricted to Indo-Europeans – it is also found amongst Mesopotamians, for instance.

There are other, less convincing examples of common mythology, derived from Proto-Indo-Europeans, such as imprisonment of essential elements of nature (sun, fire, primordial life) by evil elements and their liberation by a heroic god, which constitutes a beginning of the known world.

One religious characteristic that is clear by its absence from this Proto-religion is an ethical system. In all known Indo-European societies this evolved much later – the Neo-Platonism of the Graeco-Roman world, the fanatically obeyed law code of the early Romans or the more flexible law of the Scandinavians. In all these cases there was a marked philosophical discontinuity between primordial religion and the ethical system that evolved in subsequent centuries – independently, one would suggest, of any elements of the Indo-European pantheon. The definition of these "secondary" systems occurred long after the relevant Indo-European culture had galloped against its neighbours.

Hinduism's answer to checking the excesses of Indo-European culture is highly evocative of Neo-Platonism. Moral Hinduism is also centred on the desirability of a righteous universe, and it consists of such general considerations rather than specific commandments chiselled in stone. There is, however, a lack of specific moral direction in the Hindu universe – the world will always be as it is. This is a very different moral stance to the Zoroastrian war of good against evil. It religious canon having been written for some eight centuries, Hinduism also retains the folklore of the bloodthirsty Indo-European cutthroats, whose hero god Indra behaves accordingly.

There was a third Indo-European religious "upgrade", designed with an ethical foundation at the outset. Buddhism, founded by an Indian prince in sixth century BC, presented a heavy counterpoint to the glorified skulduggery of the ancient Indo-European ethic – and to the strident optimism and utilitarianism of Zarathushtra.

Like Zoroastrianism, Buddhism is very much a product of its environment – by now a stagnant, caste-riven society with an enormous discrepancy between rich and poor. It is ruled by inbred and effete descendants of the long-gone robber barons, who do nothing to deserve the grudging respect one could feel for the exploits of their marauding forefathers. Buddha's world, in whose realities his philosophy is rooted, cannot be repaired through righteous struggle. Buddha's solution was to withdraw from it.

As consolation to the downtrodden masses, Buddhism can be invaluable. But it struggles for relevance in a technological society with advanced social support and effective administration of justice, which in return require quality labour and participation in government from its citizen.

It is a matter of record that Judaism, Christianity, Buddhism and Islam that shape modern world also "snap-froze" the specific historical circumstances in which they were shaped.

Judaism underwent its final revision in the immediate aftermath of Judea being destroyed not once but twice, fifty years apart, followed by the final scattering of Jews into a worldwide diaspora – where avoidance of conflict with indigenous authority was paramount to survival.

Paul of Tarsus, who holds the patent on Christianity as a marketable creed, was well aware of the need to give customers what they wanted. He had to reinvent a creed that believed preached an apocalyptic showdown into something acceptable to Roman society, not to mention Roman authority. Paul had to do this at a time when Jews were not only roundly derided for their aloofness and strange practices, but also aroused automatic suspicion and distaste, being recent perpetrators of a rebellion that three Roman legions barely managed to contain.

As we look with awe on the might of modern Israel, it cannot be more obvious that Paul grafted meekness onto Messianic Judaism – to dispel, as much as he could, the Roman fear of the Jewish proclivity to rise against oppressors.

Meekness is entirely foreign to Jewish ethic. Jesus would not have preached meekness – or He would be considered insane by His audience.

The Pauline creed presents a major conundrum to its followers in a modern world replete with violence. Fortunately, few Christians ever took their religion seriously when it came to a good fight. Instead they spread their culture by sword and Gatling gun, battleship and supersonic jet. The Roman church ran the longest-lived and the most brutal totalitarian regime ever known. This remains a severe impediment to its credibility.

Likewise, Islam was always less a religion than a code of conduct for a militarized society, whose destiny was nothing less than global domination. Being a heavily syncretic religion, Islam is easy to usurp for whatever self-seeking purpose one holds dear. Unlike their Indo-European equivalents, few Islamic reformers were preoccupied with linking their religion to an effective practice of social justice or curtailment of its violent tendencies.

The deficiency of this approach was never more obvious than today, when most citizens of the Islamic world live much as they did when forces of Islam conquered their lands – a unique but dubious achievement of a faith that paints itself as the champion of the underdog.

The bellicosity of Islamic fanatics not only keeps

their world miserable and poor, but exposes fellow Muslims to the deadly wrath of the West. Many Western leaders salivate for a pretext to finish the centuries-old conflict with Islam in a classic Indo-European way: extermination of armed opposition, followed up with cultural genocide. The requisite technical means have never been more accessible – and the temptation never greater.

In contrast to these religions, the Zoroastrian creed comes without an expiry date. It was formulated at the dawn of developed society – ancient, let alone modern.

Unlike Christianity, it did not have to kowtow to the Roman colossus. It was not constructed as a religion of world conquerors, the destiny Mohammed assigned to the Arab nation.

The thrust of Zoroastrian ethics incises much deeper into the nature of post-Neolithic society than any religion formed in later, more complex social and political environments. The local factors that operate in such societies caused all latter creeds to be born with features that made them attractive at the time – but these features turned into severe disadvantages when prevailing circumstances changed.

Zoroastrianism addresses issues that go much deeper than common forms of social organization. It is a crucial question whether the principles it recommends continue to perform when carries into more advanced society, and we will examine evidence concerning this in later chapters.

In general, however, the basic principles of choosing good over evil, respect for one's society and ecology, decency and productivity had not lost their relevance in three and a half millennia, and there is no reason to expect that they ever will.

Cross-pollination in early monotheism?

Both Moses and Zarathushtra had taken the same monumental step forward – both saw God as an Almighty Being who demanded not only obedience, but also justice and decency according to divinely revealed laws.

Their God did not take over the universe by slaughtering his Father, but by creating it from the void. He cares for His creation, suffers for it and strives to preserve it. Good people need not appease Him to avert acts of sadistic petulance on His part, nor do they need to buy His grudging favours.

Did Zarathushtra and Moses cross paths? The recent revision in the probable dates for both individuals, or, at least, the origins of religions attributed to both, brings them suspiciously close together – yet it seems that Zarathushtra was the elder by up to two centuries.

I ask You, tell me truly, Lord. Who is the highest creator and father of righteousness? Who set the sun and the stars in their paths? Who makes the moon wax and wane? I am, Wise One, keen to know all this and more.

(Gathas: ix)

Yahweh said to him, "Who made man's mouth? Or who makes one mute, or deaf, or seeing, or blind? Isn't it I, Yahweh? Now therefore go, and I will be with your mouth,

(Exodus: 11-12)

It is tempting to imagine that Zarathushtra influenced a man many consider the spiritual inspiration of Moses.

The rebel Pharaoh Akhenaten had abolished the Egyptian pantheon and replaced it, albeit only for the duration of his reign, with a supreme sun god Akhen, "promoted" from the former sun god Ra, formerly of equal rank to his fellow gods. There is an interesting resemblance between Akhenaten's surviving hymns and the Gathas.

Akhenaten's reforms did not outlast him for the reason he instituted them – a vast industry of priests dedicated to various gods was made redundant overnight. As core of Egyptian technocracy, they were unlikely to go without a fight. They mounted a counter-revolution after Akhenaten's death, when they orchestrated a wholesale pogrom against the temples, cities, people and ideas that stemmed from Akhenaten's monotheistic redaction.

In destroying and cursing all reminders of his reign, they made an outstanding contribution to world heritage. An enormous library of clay tablets was found under a foundation of a building in Akhenaten's new capital, destroyed and abandoned after his death.

Known as the Amarna documents, these priceless texts, many repeating their contents in a number of languages, were thrown into the building rubble. Presumably, they were so discarded after being transcribed onto official papyrus, which had since become the dust of millennia. Destiny can have a very poignant sense of humour.

Certainly, Akhenaten and Zarathushtra lived but a stone's throw away by modern reckoning, and in ancient times a journey from Egypt to Iran was not an impossible undertaking. Akhenaten came to power as Egypt emerged from centuries of upheaval caused by the Hyksos invasion, following which many of the newcomers settled in Northern Egypt. It is not inconceivable that amongst these invaders, whose military ways smell very Indo-European, were a few followers of Zoroastrian creed.

A recent revision in Egyptian chronology suggests that Moses may have antedated Akhenaten after all – but this is something of a guess, since the Exodus does not appear to have taken place on the scale described in the Bible. Rather, a relatively small number of Jews appears to have left Egypt to rejoin those who never left Canaan. Moses may have been a very real figure, however.

There is a marked similarly in the codes of Moses and Zarathushtra. Alas, both Judaism and Zoroastrianism arose in preliterate societies, whose proceedings were largely ignored by their more advanced neighbours. The short answer has to be that we cannot ever know whether one contributed to the other. Yet, there are no other instances of monotheism in the entire human history save the Egyptian-Judaic and the Iranian. It is tall order to assume that such radical concepts evolved completely independently, less than two thousand miles from each other and at around the same time to boot.

There is no question that a latter encounter between two faiths, in the aftermath of Cyrus' conquest of Babylon, caused a heavy revision of the Judaic creed along Zoroastrian lines. Pre-exile Hebrew faith, as evidenced by the bulk of the Hebrew Bible, shows little concern for the after-life and it says nothing about a pending apocalypse. Apart from a near-total lack of eschatology (belief in the Messianic resolution at the end of the world), early Judaism is also entirely devoid of dualism – the Satan of early Hebrew Bible is a figure pithily described as an auditor, rather than a determined enemy of God.

After encounter with Persian culture, however, Judaism is seen to acquire a vague belief in after-life that was very similar to that of Zoroastrians, who avoided the error of latter religions, who promised too much in the afterlife.

Entirely Zoroastrian is the latter Judaic motif of good struggling against evil until the very end of the world, when good will eventually triumph. Today the concept of a Messiah is considered entirely Jewish – but it came from the Persians, who had it for some millennium prior to meeting the Jews.

That concept – of the present world ending with the arrival of a sanctified figure who will lead the good into triumphant assault on the forces of evil – has dominated the thoughts of one late Jewish sect, the Essenes. Their ideas on these subjects were transcribed into Christianity almost verbatim, as we now know from the materials the Essenes had penned. These are full of concepts once considered Christian innovations, but written well before the birth of Jesus. Hence the despicable scandal of the Dead Sea Scrolls, concealed from the world for forty years on Vatican's orders.

There was one other major difference – it was not until exposure to Achaemenid Persians that Judaism became an ethical system instead of a legal codex. Until then the Ten Commandments were a list of laws, not a morality with a self-evident theoretical foundation.

The God of Moses was very specific about what He wanted, but with little inclination to explain His thoughts. There were a lot of do's and don't's, rather than principles of universal justice, due process, ecology or resistance to the forces of entropy and chaos. The followers of Moses are hard put to understand why they should pass up pork and lobster, and such lack of theoretical foundation renders the Mosaic code hollow.

There are more serious contradictions. How can it be, for instance, that Thou Shalt Not Kill, when God Himself orders His followers to commit genocide in Canaan? And what of simple self-defence?

God who reveals Himself in the first three books of the Hebrew Bible does not preside over a world of good and evil. Having defined what He expects from His worshippers, God instead classifies miscreants into three groups – those who are forgiven, those who are punished and then forgiven – and those beyond forgiveness, marked for extermination.

Early Hebrews do not become good when they worship Him – nor do they become evil when they turn back to idols. They remain the same people, who are in turn loved and punished by a jealous and exclusive God. There are no good and evil creatures, merely good and evil deeds. This world view was very much the norm amongst ancient cultures in whose shadow Judaism arose – Egypt and Mesopotamia.

Nor, in fact, is Mosaic Judaism monotheistic. God who leads His flock out of Egypt does not say that He is alone – *Adonai Eloheinu, Adonai Ehad* (Our Lord Who is But One) of the daily

Hebrew prayer, is a much later formula. The God of Moses simply says that He is supreme, which is not a great advance on ordinary polytheism of the day – every ancient culture nominated a chief deity. There are even places missed by latter editors of the Hebrew Bible, where God refers to Himself in pleural form.

The God of Moses is unusual because He demands rejection of other gods – most religions of the ancient world had no quarrel with the concept that a foreign or a rival god is still a god.

Likewise, the codification of religious law is somewhat unusual, but we know that Egyptians had a complex legal system, much integrated with their religious concepts. In all likelihood, belonging to an old and wise civilization, the Egyptians were wary of chiselling laws in stone. Hammurabi, on the other hand, did so unfathomably early – around 1750 BC.

Even after Moses Judaism is still a long way from the integrated view of the world with God on one side and Satan on the other, a religious tradition we take for granted today. But it only came after contact with Persians.

Another Persian idea that was entirely absent from pre-exile Judaism is that the world will end with the arrival of a saviour, who will usher in a fair world. The belief in Messiah that is now an integral motif in Judaism was a source of great comfort to generations of Jews shut in their ghettoes throughout the Middle Ages. But it is not without cost – many Jews, like many Muslims today, lost countless lives following various self-proclaimed saviours, usually psychopaths who led their people to a certain and totally avoidable destruction.

Inspired by messianic beliefs, the great Jewish rebellion against the Romans cost Jews their country. It was entirely unnecessary, being started over minor provocation. They objected to Greeks sacrificing birds in front of a synagogue in Caesaria, built by the Romans as their provincial capital – a mainly pagan city, where such scenes must have been commonplace.

Jerusalem and the sacred Temple that stood for six centuries were razed, and Josephus puts the national toll of the rebellion at 1.1 million Jews. That may be an appealing round figure – but Judea was certainly decimated and ceased to be a viable region for the next three centuries.

The reputation of Jews in the Roman world changed from quaint to obnoxious. Emperor Hadrian, touring the ruins of Jerusalem sixty years later, did not feel much need for diplomacy. He gave Jews a genuine cause for a rebellion by proposing to rebuild Jerusalem as a cosmopolitan centre in which Jews were a minority. That provoked a second rebellion, after which Judea was razed to shards. The population was exiled with few exceptions, and Jews lost control over ancestral land.

There was never the slightest possibility that a rebellion would induce or force the Romans to abandon Judea, a vital land bridge between Egypt and Mesopotamia, especially during the centuries of conflict on the eastern frontier. The Judean rebels proved spectacularly effective militarily, but Rome had unassailable superiority in resources and numbers. How Romans dealt with rebellious provinces was well-known. All of this makes the instigators war criminals.

Equally, failure to fence off the position of Messiah from opportunists is costing Muslims dearly today. The actions of a few deranged fanatics had put the entire Islamic world on a target map of the West – an ancient enemy armed to the teeth and itching for action after six decades of relative inactivity of the Cold War.

There is a remarkable similarity between the anti-Western rantings of modern Islamic extremists and the anti-Roman rantings in the Dead Sea scroll known as the War Rule.

There is evidence that messianic ideology did little for Iranians as well. One reason for the bloodbath and the vandalism perpetrated by Arab invaders in Iran is that Zoroastrians resisted long after the fact of occupation. Uprisings, guerilla wars and passive resistance continued for nearly a century – a degree of opposition Arabs encountered nowhere else until they got across the Pyrenees.

All occupiers turn savage when confronted with ongoing opposition – it may be argued that belief in the ultimate victory of good over evil is all very well, but it should be tempered with a little patience.

Zoroastrianism as a social force

It is now pertinent to examine the effect of Zoroastrianism on Realpolitik. Did it ever make a social difference? Was Zoroastrian society ever better than its neighbours? Was it stronger? Was it more honourable?

We know all about societies forged by Christians, Buddhists, Hindus, Muslims and Jews. Each religion (as known today) constrains its followers to a particular moral code. In theory, each religion should impose a distinct influence on society where it is practised by the power elite, if not the majority of the population.

History suggests that many heads of state pay homage to religion, but that cannot be used as proof of their pious nature. The positive aspects of religion seldom restrain the base instincts of rulers and their henchmen. The question is whether Zoroastrian values improved Zoroastrian society in other ways.

Zoroastrianism first became an historically verifiable entity during Achaemenid era. It can be said that only adherence to Zoroastrian values explains the unusually "modern" behaviour of Cyrus as a conqueror – his well-documented tolerance of the cultures of conquered people, aversion to destruction and emphasis on human dignity and natural justice – so "modern", in fact, that no modern society has yet implemented his code in full. Acts of ruthlessness typical of an ancient tyrant are few and far in between in the life of Cyrus:

The thought once occurred to us how many republics have been overthrown by people who preferred to live under any form of government other than a republican, and again, how many monarchies and how many oligarchies in times past have been abolished by the people. We reflected, moreover, how many of those individuals who have aspired to absolute power have either been deposed once for all and that right quickly; or if they have continued in power, no matter for how short a time, they are objects of wonder as having proved to be wise and happy men.[...] Thus, as we meditated on this analogy, we were inclined to conclude that for man, as he is constituted, it is easier to rule over any and all other creatures than to rule over men. But when we reflected that, who reduced to obedience a vast number of men and cities and nations, we were then compelled to change our opinion and decide that to rule men might be a task neither impossible nor even difficult, if one should only go about it in an intelligent manner. At all events, we know that people obeyed Cyrus willingly, although some of them were distant from him a journey of many days, and others of many months; others, although they had never seen him, and still others who knew well that they never should see him. Nevertheless they were all willing to be his subjects. (Cyropaedia of Xenophon; The Life of Cyrus The Great, Xenophon)

The famous Behistun inscription of Darius I, the successor and nephew of Cyrus, leaves no doubt that he was either a devout Zoroastrian or wanted to be seen as one. It is reasonably safe to state that all successors of Darius either accepted or genuinely followed the same religion. It is safe, however, to say that Zoroastrianism must have been known by that time.

Darius I was not called "the Great" for nothing. His reign was marked by spectacular successes on all fronts. He inherited a swathe of freshly conquered territories, and he left his successors a highly organized administration. We have few actual facts about his personal behaviour, but the Behistun text is certainly suggestive of a high degree of personal integrity, in image if not in reality. The remainder of what we know about his personal behaviour comes from Herodotus, who also paints a flattering picture.

Conversion of Iranian kings to Zoroastrianism certainly appears to be complete by the time of Darius I, but Achaemenid Persia never abandoned religious tolerance. As we saw earlier, that could have been the case because Zoroastrianism was the religion of Achaemenid elite, rather than a populist state religion.

Under Darius' successors the empire went from strength to strength. It was lightly ruled by distant kings who seemed to have a reasonable grasp on the concept of due process: the locals were ruled by satraps who themselves risked summary justice if caught abusing their power. The effectiveness of the Achaemenid system of checks and balances speaks for itself through dazzling economic success.

It is not credible to suggest that Zoroastrian values played no part in that success. Operating at least at an elite level, such values would have provided considerable extra stability and security in the Persian society. Subscription, if not fanatical adherence, to the principle of natural justice, is at the heart of the success of most modern democracies, and it is likely that the same principle had a similar effect in the Achaemenid era.

Achaemenid Persia was an economic and cultural tour de force. It dazzled Greek neighbours, who left lengthy records of their jealousy to posterity. They especially noted the orderliness of Persian society, and Greeks minced no words, directly attributing this quality to the Persian religion.

Six hundred years before Christ the Persian Empire enjoyed almost modern-style means of communicating over its vast expanse. The Suez Canal has been dug (by order of Darius I), and the world expanded even further through the eager efforts of Persian vassals, the Phoenicians.

Whilst the military was poorly organized and coordinated, Egypt succumbed to Persian rule and caused little trouble. There were rumbles on the northern frontiers, in the form of harassment from nomadic Iranians (indeed, Cyrus lost his life in one such conflict) – but these were no threat to the body of the empire, and the nomadic frontier was gradually pushed further and further away from the heartland. The first expedition into insolent Greece resulted in temporary success, the Acropolis being burnt and plundered by the Persian army under Xerxes I.

It may be concluded that in the first of three phases, during which Iranians were ruled under the auspices of Zoroastrianism, the social influence of that religion was an unqualified success.

Cyrus the Great from a 1917 photograph of an undated Iranian painting. The image has credibility due to details of his attire.

Achaemenid society met with a sudden and a catastrophic demise at the hands of Alexander, but that is hardly a reflection on its social or economic strength. It does, however, provide a splendid example of the bias with which we view history – we call that vandal the Great, denying that epithet to Napoleon and Hitler, whose military exploits are equally worthy of note.

The Persian Empire was not a "colossus on feet of clay". That's a nice sound bite, but no colossus can exist without being militarily capable.

Alexander's victory has to be put in perspective. He had never actually lost a single campaign, and being vanquished by his army says nothing about the prowess of his opponents or the viability of their society. Alexander was a superbly talented predator whose personal acquaintance with Aristotle should not be confused with intellectual or ethical development. As Bertrand Russell remarked, the transcontinental bloodbath is a predictably sad outcome of teaching philosophy to cutthroats.

What Alexander mainly remembered from Aristotle's efforts amounted to an ideology of Greek supremacy, according to which cultural genocide was a desirable act. Alexander used that ideology as he did any weapon at his disposal – to maximize the ratio of carnage to effort.

Alexander's mission to avenge Greece and to

spread the supposedly superior Hellenic creed became the most extreme example of an Indo-European blitzkrieg – a whirlwind military assault by a small expeditionary force that smashed aside local resistance from Asia Minor all the way into India, Mesopotamia and Egypt.

His victims were not savages but ancient cultures whose heritage pre-dated that of the Greeks – Persians, Indians, Babylonians Phoenicians, Judeans and Egyptians. The net result of Alexander's exploits was the loss, rather than gain, of humanity's intellectual property.

Alexander created a quasi-Hellenic empire over a vast stretch of Eurasia in a mere space of two decades, with barely enough soldiers to fill a significant football stadium of today. That his empire fractured into three parts after his death is largely a result of his sudden demise. Two out of three parts became entirely functional, powerful and long-lived states.

Alexander's cultural blitzkrieg was also a great success, even after restoration of native rule in deeply anti-Hellenic cultures such as Judea and Parthia. From what we know their customs and arts, they remained recognizably influenced by Hellenic civilization all the way into India. There was an undeniable benefit from this cross-cultural pollination, especially in Egypt. But its benefits are seen in very different light when one considers the loss of entire Persian literature.

Thousands of ox hides had burned in the royal palace at Susa, with many more less famously destroyed elsewhere.

Equally, there is little profit in revisionisms about the "Accursed Iskander", as voiced by modern Iranians. Alexander beat his opponents fair and square – in the case of Persia, the campaign consisted of a series of victories, won against vastly superior numbers by his tactical genius and the superb quality of his troops. He was a true Indo-European chieftain of old who fought at the head of his troops and, even by accounts of hostile observers, did so with great valour. The ugly personal traits, which he did not see fit to conceal, were entirely irrelevant to the fact of his absolute military success. He vanquished all, weak and strong.

We apply a double standard when we accept the Greek assessment of Alexander's victory over Persians. To Greeks the eventual outcome was never in doubt – such was their perceived cultural superiority over "barbarian" Persia.

We, who are raised to admire Greek culture, are taught that Alexander's idea of a world becoming a Greek commonwealth was a noble, messianic mission. In reality it was little more than another burst of Indo-European aggression, most of it at the expense of weaker Indo-Europeans.

In fact, dispassionate analysis shows that cultural

sophistication does not always translate into military strength. Indeed, an enlightened attitude to human life is a distinct disadvantage: witness the ignominious usurpation of Greece by "barbarian" Romans, the dismantling of the Western Roman Empire by Huns and Germanic tribes, the devastating sweep of Arab armies that took them from Mecca into the heart of Europe within a span of one century, the calamity visited on both East and West by Mongols and again by Turks.

Objectively speaking, the only place where forcible institution of Greek ideals yielded worthwhile results was Egypt. Its stagnant culture and a moribund economy were revived by injection of intellectual vigour and a sudden influx of foreign trade.

The rest of Alexander's victims remember him only as a destroyer, Iranians very much so – and so should we, lest we spawn more Alexanders.

The Parthian Federation

Iran disappears from Western eyes after Alexander's rampage.

The fellow Indo-Europeans who decapitated the Achaemenid Empire were aggressive cultural hegemonists who hated all things Persian – with some reason. Iranian culture survived only because the invaders did not have the means to destroy it, as we may well imagine they wanted to do. We know that around the same time Alexander's successors also attempted a cultural genocide in Judea, and we know that it was thwarted by a sheer miracle.

Today we can only imagine how different the world would have looked if the Phoenician culture survived and continued to contribute to humanity. Punic Wars had resulted in the erasure of its colonies, and Alexander wiped out its cities in Phoenician homeland.

Persia barely missed out on sharing the Phoenicians' fate. It is possible that Alexander may have destroyed many native cultures had he lived longer – but some were easier than others to erase.

Phoenicians made the mistake of housing their empire in small seaside strongholds supplied from the sea, from which they were able to intimidate and repel native aggressors. Alas, these strongholds were no match for the armies of Alexander and Scipio. It was much harder to perpetrate genocide of that kind in Iran, whose territory took months for any army to traverse.

We may speculate that during the "silent centuries" of Iranian history – 160 years after the Macedonian conquest – life in Iranian provinces went on more or less as before, including the continuity of religious practices, with or without Greek approval. Even before Alexander most of the Iranian landscape simply could not support a large population, let alone an army of the size required to fully subjugate the former empire and to set up the kind of police state one would require to stamp out an established religion.

The native populations of Macedonia and Greece were nowhere near large enough to replace Iranians with a colonists. Whilst neither Alexander nor his Asian inheritors, the Seleucid family, were above ordering a genocide, they shrunk away from the economic ruin that would bring to their new domain.

As ever, economics and military considerations were intricately intertwined. Within only two centuries after Alexander the Seleucid army was entirely composed of mercenaries. The Seleucids could afford mercenaries to defend themselves, but they could not afford to use mercenaries to inflict damage on their productive population.

Alexander himself had no choice – his thirty-thousand-strong army was as large a movement of people as the terrain could support. The landscape of Asia Minor was particularly useless without those who made that land productive. Even Alexander could see that interference with indigenous structures would cost him dearly.

Large armies are a product of a modern economy that can afford to deliver supplies to an army on the march. They are also a product of modern civil engineering, which allows such concentration of humanity to proceed with little loss. As late as sixteenth century AD only a third of all military casualties was incurred in actual battle – the rest died of diseases acquired in army camps, bunched for fortification into unhygienic trash heaps that simply begged for epidemics.

Without doubt, artefacts of Persian culture were deliberately targeted on a mass scale, but even Alexander was unhappy to hear that one of his whores set fire to the Emperor's palace – which was, after all, now his.

Less than two hundred years after Alexander's death and at, approximately, the same time, the rule of the Seleucids was thrown off in both Judea and Iran. After defeating Greek mercenaries both Jews and Iranians founded states, ruled by the military leaders who achieved liberation.

Secessionist effort by Parthians, a tribe from the north of old Persian empire, began as early as 250 BC. These have reached incontrovertible significance by 164 BC, definitively ending by 129 BC, when Parthians pushed their frontier to the Tigris river and established Ctesiphon (near the more modern Baghdad) as the winter capital.

We do not have a lot of information about the origins of the Iranian revolt. But a good idea of what motivated it can be gained from the study of the Maccabean movement in Judea.

Before the Maccabean revolt (167 – 165 BC) Judea was a token Jewish enclave, a few hundred miles across at the most. Its population could not have been more than a hundred thousand, and it could not possibly have wielded more than ten thousand men.

The success of Maccabean forces over the Greeks is a most impressive feat of guerilla warfare, but it proves little apart, possibly, from divine assistance in their struggle. What it says loudly is that Seleucids lost much of their formal strength and were unable to maintain a grip on their domain. Such a defeat was unthinkable in Alexander's day.

Things may have been harder for Iranian rebels, who were closer to the Seleucid home base (modern Syria and Iraq), but the Iranians rode a wave of resurgent nationalism. Gone were the days when manic Alexander intoxicated hungry veterans to march from one wild success to the next. The Seleucids paid mercenaries to maintain control over conquered territory, and their enemy fought under the banner of resurrected national pride. Such ideological edge can dramatically alter the balance of forces, as the wars of modern Israel attest each way.

After a century of low-level confrontation the Parthians had the measure of Greek armies. They discovered how to deal with the Macedonian phalanx, a formation that took Alexander around the known world without a single defeat. Invented by his father, it consisted of a box formed by rows of men with *sarissae*, very long pikes carried in two pieces and assembled like modern tent poles before battle. Whilst relatively awkward to manoeuvre, the phalanx was irresistable in frontal assault, anything in its way being trampled down and demolished by a moving hedge of spear points. The *phalangoi* locked shields to defend against arrow volleys, and they could plant the butts of their pikes to form a barrier insurmountable to chariots and ordinary cavalry.

But Iranians discovered something else. That technical advance underpinned the national revival of the Parthian era – the evolution of what Europeans call a knight, an armoured rider mounted on an armoured horse.

Originally invented by Alans, an Iranian tribe still found on the edge of the Caucasus, full armour was enthusiastically adopted by neighbouring Parthians, who quickly realized that being fully armoured afforded more possibilities than merely staying alive – a charge by a column of knights became a devastating assault tactic. Few armies had withstood such a charge for the next fourteen centuries, until the long bow put an end to the supremacy of armoured charge. Arabs won against an army of knights by attacking when Iran was unable to field enough of them at the right place and time. Crusaders beat Arabs because the had enough knights to form a charge, losing to Arabs when they were deprived of an opportunity to deploy knights to full effect.

The tank blitzkrieg is merely a motorized version of the same tactic. It may be said that air power is the only new development in warfare since the Parthian knight – a very effective aide to ground assault but not a substitute for one, as modern Americans proved on far too many occasions.

We know from European sources how expensive knights were to field – a twelfth century Crusader knight cost the equivalent of two modern home mortgages to equip, let alone train from youth. Yet Iranians fielded armies of such knights continuously for nine hundred years. After their debacle against Alexander, they never regained their confidence for fighting on foot, their infantry always playing an auxiliary, clean-up role.

The origin of chivalry is shrouded with mists of inadequate sources, but it is said that the code of conduct that defines a noble warrior also came from Alans along with the armour. It makes sense entirely – a force of knights was virtually unstoppable in the field. Even an individual knight represented an unstoppable danger to lesser-armed opponents, and society quickly discovered the need to restrain them with behavioural norms. The Iranian origins of chivalry are self-evident, especially the requirement that a knight remains true to his word. One is left to wonder how many of the customs taken for granted in the West are of the same origin.

In addition to knights, Parthian armies employed larger units of mounted archers, who ran up to enemy ranks at full speed and turned, shooting during the turn over their horses' rumps (a Parthian arrow became the byword for firing a damaging shot on departure). The archers refilled their quivers from camel trains stationed well away from the enemy and returned, maintaining a steady shower of arrows over the enemy. Fully armoured knights are also believed to have carried powerful bows, unlike European knights, who disdained projectile weapons.

Parthians began their battles by having lightly-armoured riders shower their enemies with arrows from a safe distance, reducing and demoralizing the opposing ranks – and then the knights charged. They would run at full gallop at the enemy from the direction of the rising sun, using raised dust to deny the enemy visual information about the depth of their column. Their armour was especially polished to a bright shine to cast blinding reflections, and the noise of the charge had the same effect as the thundering clatter of tank tracks does today.

The long pikes of Parthian knights were attached to the horse's armour by short stirrups, directed rather than fully supported by the rider (Parthian saddles were not up to the task of supporting the rider as well as stirrups, invented by Mongols). The pike was rammed through enemy ranks at full gallop, able to skewer more than one man at a time.

It takes some years of reading Western sources before one realizes that Parthian and Persian empires were, in essence, the same ethnographic entity. In fact, there was no change of ethnic identity upon assumption of power by the Parthian dynasty – the people they ruled were just the same as under Achaemenids or Seleucids.

That spiteful bit of scholarly neglect stems from the fact that Iranians soon crossed swords with another Indo-European predator and progenitor of modern world order – the Roman Empire.

Romans could not hide from it – the Iranian conflict was a running insult to successive generations of Roman arms. It was the only frontier at which Rome made no lasting progress – not in the beginning, not later, not ever. Neither force of arms nor cultural and economic seduction had any effect. There were six wars between Rome and Parthia, and only one can be considered a Roman victory.

The frontier moved back and forth. Beyond that frontier the Roman sphere of influence ended – despite the fact that Parthia was less of an empire than a loose federation, in which one regional king was recognized as having a rank above others ("king of kings"), mostly as a military commander.

One ruling Roman emperor (Valerian) became a prisoner of war in Iran. Another (Gordian), died during the campaign against the Parthians, although it is possible that he may have been assassinated. A third, Julian the Apostate, actually died after being skewered by a Parthian spear. Julian was about to undo Christianity and may have changed the course of Western history had he lived – an irony that Parthians and their descendants may have found delicious.

At its eclipse the Roman Empire was still locked in a see-saw contest with Parthians' Sassanid successors (who overthrew the Parthians in the third century AD). The running conflict with Iranians was passed to Byzantium by inheritance, which it neither welcomed nor was equipped to manage.

The Parthians were effective in their choice of tactics, honed in liberation wars against the Greeks. Anything the Romans tried against Parthian armies either proved useless right away or was effectively neutralized in short order. A good example is the Battle of Carrhae, in which a force of some 20,000 Romans were massacred by a Parthian army of one third that number. When Romans found themselves under a hail of arrows shot from a greater distance than their bows could cover, they formed up into a *testudo* ("turtle" formation in which a group formed a hemispherical shell of metal with locked shields). The Parthian knights then charged, skewering and trampling the legionaries tangled up in the *testudo*. After they passed, the disrupted formation was again showered with Parthian arrows, killing the remainder.

A mounted archer who can shoot without aim at full gallop is a weapon that cannot be easily copied. Such skills in both horse and rider are developed from a very early age. The modern revival of mounted archery is quite unequivocal on that score, even though modern saddlery allows the rider to have much more control and balance than in ancient times.

The best that Romans could do was copy the Parthian knight – copying successful ideas, admittedly, being something they did promptly and well. The Roman version was called a *clibanarium* by the Romans (originally the name of an iron field stove used by Roman legions). In due course, *clibanarii* were blended with the traditional Roman caste of equestrians, and the result of that merger is the European knight. In latter times the Greek-speaking Byzantines used the term *cataphract*. As in Iran, a knight was usually a man of means, trained for warfare from an early age and able to afford the equipment that kept him alive.

There is mixed information about whether Parthians were devout Zoroastrians. The emperor Vologeses I (ruled 51-80 AD) ordered the compilation of Zoroastrian sacred library from surviving fragments and oral tradition. A few Parthian emperors have Zoroastrian names.

A revival of Zoroastrianism makes sense at a time of a nationalistic surge. United under Iranian command for the first time in seven generations, it is likely that Iranians restored their national religion and its associated traditions to a similar position they occupied under Achaemenids. Like the latter, the Parthian rulers did not have the luxury of standardizing the religious beliefs of their subjects against their will.

The Parthian dynasty came from the north. The Parthian tribe is considered to be relatives of the Scythians – Iranian-speaking nomads living in what is now southern Ukraine. These were a warlike nomadic people considered peripheral to the culture of former Persian Empire (which subjugated them at great cost and otherwise lacked the resources to interfere in Scythian affairs). Whatever religion the Scythians chose to practise, it is most unlikely that anyone could do anything about it.

They Parthian dynasty that came to dominate the Iranian world through its overthrow of the Greeks, may have been Zoroastrians – but it is more likely that they chose to adopt it, in word if not deed, just as the Germanic tribes that forced their way into Western Roman Empire chose to adopt Christianity. The Parthian leadership united Iranians against a common enemy, and national pride was resurgent. Zoroastrianism rode that wave long and high – but not all was well when it counted the cost of being enmeshed in politics.

Being founded by a warrior nobility from the edge of the Iranian world, possibly even racially distinct from other neighbouring Iranian speakers such as Bactrians, the new empire was a very different entity. There was little love lost between Parthians and the Zoroastrian stronghold of Bactria – the second Parthian king even assisted the Seleucids in an attack on Bactrians.

The new regime had little access to the fine tools of Achaemenid governance, for 160 years have passed since the death of the last Achaemenid king. The administrative and economic fabric was now Hellenic, and much has changed, with centres of power pushed around the map by Alexander and his successors. There was no question of simply resurrecting the corpse of Alexander's victim. New ideas and means were called for.

The Parthian dynasty never even tried to set itself up as an empire in the Achaemenid style. It was always a loose federation of warrior kingdoms, and whenever a vast territory cannot be controlled by force, ideology comes into play.

It certainly would not have had the ideological inclination, or the political teeth, to enforce the practice of any particular religion. It is unlikely that in Parthian times Zoroastrianism was more than one of the religions, possibly one preferred by the ruling nobility.

Image of a Parthian general (presumed to be that of Surena, the Parthian commander at Carrhae).

An Iranian bas-relief of a Parthian knight (Sassanid era)

A Roman bas-relief (Arch of Septimus Severus, @ 200 AD) showing Parthian prisoners – an elegant portrayal of wishful thinking.

Achaemenid Empire (above) and Parthian Empire
(below)

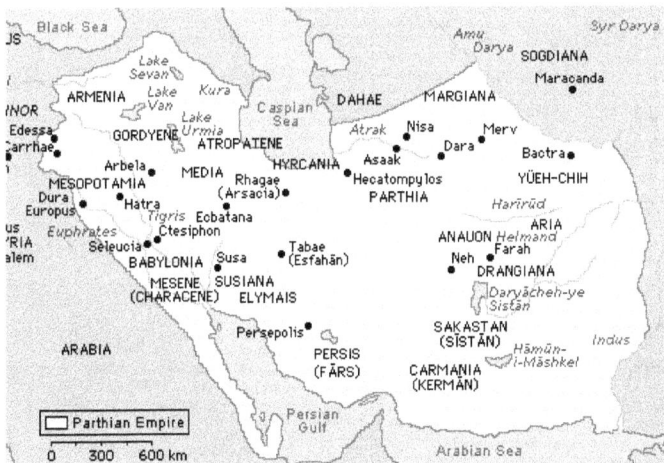

Evidence about Parthian state ideology is thin, but it must have been effective enough. Military performance is not an instant guide to the strength of the parent society, but it is difficult to fight centuries of wars against an enemy like Rome and enjoy near-constant success without being a great economic power, and it is impossible to run so many campaigns without an effective system of administration.

We know that Parthians did not have a strong central government – rather, they appear to have been governed by consent, allowing them to operate a low-overhead feudal system, with whose invention Parthia may be credited.

Feudalism has a bad name, having become a byword for oppression of the common man by upper classes. Undeniably, it results in a social pecking order – but that was not the main point.

A feudal system allows a weak central state to be powerful in war. The main purpose of feudalism is to create a hierarchical network of nobles – the evils of an unaccountable lord ruling hapless serfs being an irrelevant side effect of this system.

Without being able to oppress his noble subordinates, the king is nevertheless able to call them to arms, at their expense. The burden of state taxation is much reduced, as the central state carries virtually no overheads. It may maintain the king's court, in some cases, but little else. Each region is self-sufficient economically and administratively.

Feudalism allowed the Parthians to build their empire with virtually no money, administrative complexity or even basic literacy. It was a highly dynamic structure that allowed Iranians to concentrate resources on mowing down the Roman legions. In contrast, their enemies spent fortunes on state-run mobilization, supply lines, administration and other overheads, only to add to Parthian pride through their demise.

In his classic 1897 treatise on Parthia, George Rawlinson emphasizes that feudal systems of Parthia and Europe had more differences than similarities. With respect, that misses the point – in comparison with a large central government, both were efficient, low-cost administrative structures – except the Parthian feudalism came first, by some six hundred years.

European feudalism was heavily contaminated by church politics and the rampant addiction of Roman economy to slavery – these forces shaped the European serf in the likeness of a slave. From what we know, slavery was not unknown in Iran, but it was never the backbone of its economy.

Parthian feudalism began with the need of the emperor to call on his nobles at times of war, and each subsequent rank extended the same obligation downwards.

Europeans, if one can put it that way, formed the feudal system from the wrong end. European feudalism was born of an imperial decree bonding free men to their present professions. Then the all-powerful Roman state instituted price control over all goods and services. That caused enterprising people to move around, which the state prohibited in turn. Then reasonable individuals began to abandon unviable occupations, and that was declared unlawful as well. At that juncture the nominally free citizens of Rome found themselves more or less in the shoes of a mediaeval serf, who lingered in Europe until liberation of Russian peasants – formally in 1861, but in reality in 1993.

Given the known military, economic and political successes of Parthian society, the lack of a strong top-down system of government cries for a conclusion that something else helped to move society towards productive purpose.

It is known that Parthian troops saluted the sun before battle, but otherwise the data is too sketchy to support any forthright statements. It is reasonable to suggest that promotion of Zoroastrianism – perhaps a simplified version – was a notable element of social and national cohesion. It would have been all too easy to represent Rome as the agent of Satan, one that every righteous Parthian must help oppose on religious, as well as patriotic, grounds.

It is also likely that Zoroastrianism, a priori, was engineered into the feudal structure, much like Christianity in the early centuries of its ascendancy. It is likely that Zoroastrian clergy provided the same lay services as did the clergy in Europe – record keeping, administration, a repository of written and oral knowledge as well as basic legal and medical services.

That is what is certainly observed in the better-documented times immediately after Parthian period. This is the best one can do, as Parthians left virtually no records: assume that much of what is observed in the times of their glorious successors had its origins in the handiwork of the Parthian dynasty.

The Iranian superpower

The Parthian dynasty was overthrown by the Sassanids. Under their stewardship Iran grew into a colossus that even exceeded the high watermarks achieved in Achaemenid times in wealth, culture, administration and war.

The artefacts of that era are many, ranging from sumptuous architecture to metalwork, sculpture, coinage and jewellery. We know that Iranians became addicted to theatre and developed this art along Hellenic lines. We also know they had a powerful literary tradition. None of it survives as original texts, but Sassanid literature is referenced in too many sources to sustain the accusation of illiteracy, as levelled at their predecessors.

Unlike Parthian rulers, the Sassanid rulers built a sophisticated machine of imperial government. It was run, it appears, with much assistance from the Zoroastrian clergy, who heavily feature in legal proceedings as well as other aspects of public administration. It appears that the enmeshment of ecclesiastic establishment into power politics was every bit as complex as that of the Christian church in Imperial Rome, with secular and religious authorities using each other as they saw fit and frequently finding themselves on opposite sides in various struggles.

To the modern eye, the Sassanid emperors and lesser-ranking officials made decisions with less reference to established law than their own imprimatur. They were more prone to abuse their office than Roman emperors – but it should also be noted that the Roman emphasis on due process was exceptional in the ancient world (as Germanic countries are exceptional in this respect today). The Sassanid system was representative of the way the rest of the ancient world worked.

The Iranian emperor reigned supreme. No ruler of Iran had ever been humiliated in public. In contrast, one Roman emperor had the ignominy of standing outside a cathedral in rags, having to beg forgiveness for his misdeeds from the local bishop.

It would be naïve to suggest that Zoroastrian principles precluded systemic corruption, but it does seem that those found guilty of wrong-doing in office were punished with greater indignation. Sassanid attitudes to corrupt behaviour were not those of contemporary Egypt or India, where abuse of power was seen as unavoidable, if theoretically illegal, and where corruption too outrageous to ignore was punished with an air of fatigue, rather than ire at violation of a higher principle.

Sassanid Iran also boasted a powerful scientific establishment, manifest by what Arabs found and largely preserved. After Arab conquest Iran remained a powerhouse of literature, visual art, science and engineering. Its artistic tradition even survived the Moslem injunction against graven images, becoming the Persian school of miniature, found in numerous Islamic manuscripts.

Avicenna (Abu Sinna) was an Iranian, as was Al-Biruni. Iranian poetry, as illustrated by the epic Shah Nameh, became the foundation of classical Arab poetry. Iranian architecture became standard throughout the Islamic world. Even today Iran boasts a vibrant culture that is, in many respects, a flag-bearer among Islamic nations.

We have considerable information about maritime exploration under the Sassanids, who ventured far and wide in the quest for trade. Most of the tales that make up A Thousand and One Nights are not Arabic but Iranian in origin. Seafaring was already well-established under Achaemenids, much enhanced by Phoenician vassalage – Phoenicians were consummate sailors, who already circumnavigated Africa in prehistoric times. The Sassanid era saw extensive trade throughout the Indian Ocean, with Sassanid coins and other artefacts found from India to Zanzibar.

Iran made much use of the artery now known as the Silk Road, taxing its traffic as well as enjoying extensive cultural and commercial exchange with China. There were extensive contacts with the Chinese even in Parthian times: enough Parthians resettled in China to have a typical surname, starting with a prefix "An" to indicate their Parthian ancestry.

The customs of Iranian nobility and courts, as well as their cuisine and entertainment, were widely emulated in the Western world, especially even before after the collapse of the Roman power in the West empire.

Overall, we are left to guess how many elements of the Sassanid culture our culture takes for granted. Most of the original sources had not survived, but the legacy of Sassanian Iran was nevertheless perpetuated by Byzantines and Arabs, plagiarized without acknowledgement.

It can be safely concluded that Zoroastrian Iran was a spectacularly powerful and effective society, at least when it came to application of force – by then a particularly expensive enterprise. Iran remained demonstrably capable of major military actions until abruptly decapitated, at an opportune moment, by the armies of Islam in the seventh century AD.

The remnant of that splendour had survived and even returned to glory under Islamic rule. Alas, an even greater disaster arrived in the thirteenth century: the Mongols had ravaged the social fabric of Iran even more than they changed the character and destiny of Russia.

It is a fact (not necessarily of a causal nature) that the Zoroastrian phase of Iranian history outshone the era of Achaemenid and Parthian ecumenicism. After religious revival Iran was clearly a more viable society. No one can accuse the Sassanid Empire of being a "colossus with clay feet", even though its decapitation was just as abrupt as that of the Achaemenid Empire.

The founder of the Sassanid dynasty was actually said to be a Zoroastrian priest, and Sassanid Empire became a theocracy in which the law of Zarathushtra applied in full – an interesting precursor to the republic of Iranian ayatollahs.

We know that in Sassanid times priests, who also served as lawyers and legal advisors to the king, formed a dictatorial clique. They left a very messy legacy that doesn't quite make the Catholic Church look pure – but does indeed make Roman machinations look mundane.

We know that for the first time Zoroastrians began to persecute those of other faiths, such as Christians and Jews. As tool of power, therefore, Zoroastrianism appears to be no vaccine against corruption or hatred.

But whilst Zoroastrian Iran had worked up a hefty reputation as a dangerous enemy, a civilization replete with sophistication and a prodigious generator of wealth, the creed of Zarathushtra paid a heavy toll for becoming an official religion.

Selling a monotheistic religion to the public of late antiquity was always a complex proposition – witness the Hebrew Bible's numerous laments about idol worship. God and Abraham had signed a tight contract that completely forbade the worship of other Gods. Idolatry was punishable by death according to Jewish law (that is, if a thunderbolt didn't get to you first), yet we know from archaeological evidence that idol worship and even human sacrifice continued to be practised in Judea, within clear sight of the Temple.

One is forced to conclude that while most Jewish kings had the muscle to eradicate such practices on their territory, they did not have the political power to antagonize their polytheistic subjects.

Likewise, the Sassanid elevation of Zoroastrianism to the status of official religion was achieved at the price of a compromise – its abstract nature was diluted with pagan elements. The ancient mindset was naturally polytheistic, even though the modern thinker has trouble even imagining multiple gods. Such mindset cannot be changed by decree, even at the point of a sharp sword.

The ensuing reform borrowed from a more

ancient version of Iranian religion. As mentioned, it is possible that such polytheism existed alongside Zoroastrianism all along, and the Sassanids compromised by fusing both religions, rather than engage in costly persecutions. A sudden break with the old tradition does indeed carry a heavy toll – witness the state-sponsored reform of the Russian Orthodox Church four hundred years ago, from which Russian orthodoxy is still recovering.

The old Iranian religion (which, after all, was a close geographic and cultural relative to the Greek) did indeed allow Hellenic residents of Iran to feel more at home – a creator god, a god of thunder, war and punishment, who rebels against the creator god and dethrones him in some unpleasant manner, and a female deity of goodness, fertility and other related sentiments.

This is referred to as Zurvanism, practised throughout the Sassanid era, although there were more fundamentalist and entirely heretical offshoots as well. Father Time (Greek Chronos) was represented by his Iranian equivalent of Zurvan.

A softer, feminine deity called Anahita was resurrected to provide a caring, humane counterpart to the main dualist deities. Anahita worship occupied approximately the same niche as the cult of Virgin Mary in mediaeval Europe. Ahura Mazda was skewed (and somewhat demoted) to resemble the Greek Zeus along righteous Zoroastrian lines. Angra Mainu, the Zoroastrian Satan, got the best deal from Zurvanist reform – he remained essentially the same. This is no coincidence, as there is no essentially malevolent god in the Greek pantheon – no Greek god has a monopoly on malevolence or malice.

The Zurvanist variant did not survive the collapse of Zoroastrian society, being an obvious departure from the original stem of Zoroastrian thought, which many Zoroastrians may have resented. Overall, the Zurvanist period may be seen as a dead end – inculcation of the ecclesiastic hierarchy with secular power, dilution of monotheism and abuse of secular power for persecution of rival religions and alternative versions of dualism itself. Zurvanism played a clear role in the downfall of Zoroastrianism.

Ironically, it was during this period when Zoroastrianism again began to export itself. It was never a proselytizing religion – unlike Christians or Muslims, its followers were never obligated to spread it by word or sword.

The first foreigners that visibly adopted Zoroastrian elements (whilst still retaining its separate identity) were the Jews mired in Babylonian exile. Their banishment from Judea was rescinded by Cyrus, who also ordered the

Jerusalem Temple to be rebuilt with Babylonian funds. All elements of the messianic doctrine – the end of the world, confrontation between good and evil, the ultimate and final triumph of the good – are Zoroastrian in origin. These themes emerge in the Hebrew Bible only after the Persian period.

Early Christianity adopted many Zoroastrian elements, both directly and through its native Jewish tradition. The Christian heaven, purgatory and hell were already accepted by the Jews, although afterlife was never fully entrenched into mainstream Judaism. It remains a contentious topic to this day, with many Orthodox Jews believing in no afterlife at all, other than eternal rest and eternal memory of the deceased. There is an interesting hiatus in that doctrine, with the Persian-style belief that the souls of all deceased will be resurrected by the Messiah. But there is no consistent explanation as to where these souls are parked in the meanwhile.

The canonical literature of Judaism contains many attempts to settle this issue. But at the end of the day, mainstream Jews stick to the original precept that one is to make full use of life because it is the only one that is given for certain. The Iranian graft has not taken, in other words – in strong contrast to the centrality of afterlife dogma amongst Christians and Muslims, who are entirely content to ruin this world in expectation of the next.

Satan is another important Zoroastrian element that did not cut much ice with Jews. In contrast, dualism exerted a strong, seldom acknowledged influence on early Christian theoreticians, such as Augustine.

The Dead Sea materials dated from second century BC demonstrate that most of the (Zoroastrian) elements, attributed to Christianity as improvements on Judaism, have been prevalent in Jewish thought long before Jesus. Some may have been more prominent than they are now, or they may have existed as apocrypha – quasi-religious folklore, taken more seriously by some sects than others.

It is likewise evident that Mohammed used the familiar and available Jewish and Christian sources, rather than directly from the more distant Iranian creed, but he would have known where they came from. Zoroastrians appeared to have had a mystique – witness the story about the three Magi who came to adore the newborn Jesus. Also witness the spread of Mithraism, the Roman version of Iranian dualism. Ancient Jews may have impressed their neighbours with their staunch faith, but Sassanid Iranians had the culture, the wealth and the combat record to impress on a global scale.

Mithraism was a Roman cult with a prominent

behavioural code modelled on Zoroastrianism. It was popular amongst and exclusive to serving and retired members of the Roman army, which came to include the Roman oligarchy. Mithraists left very few records apart from temples, built in cellars and often sealed intact during destruction of the buildings above them.

From what has been reconstructed, Mithraism placed heavy emphasis on a rigid moral code and a world view with strong dualistic polarity, essentially along the lines of fundamentalist Zoroastrianism. However, it also had heavy overtones of Freemason-style ritual, secrecy and social networking. The best-documented ritual appeared to involve a sacrifice of a bull, mimicking an ancient Indo-European tradition reflected in Zoroastrian folklore, wherein the slaughter of a primaeval bull gives origin to all things living. There was also a strong emphasis on the sun and the sacred flame. Yet Mithra appeared to be worshipped as the traditional Roman Jupiter, rather than as an abstract Ahura Mazda.

Mithra was the pre-Zoroastrian god of victory in the Indo-Iranian pantheon, whom Zarathushtra downgraded to an Archangel Michael-style figure. Indeed, the latter received such prominence in the early days of Christianity because of the need to absorb large numbers of Mithraists, to whom this was sold as a mere change in name. The sale was successful – Mithraism vanished shortly after Roman Empire adopted Christianity as state religion. Mithraists knew how to obey orders.

By the time of Constantine, the emperor – usually a former general – was also the titular head of the Mithraic cult. To this we owe the date of Christmas: Romans celebrated the winter solstice on the twenty-fifth day of December. Mithraists such as Constantine, who pinned Christmas to that date, celebrated the return of the sun as the holiest day in the calendar.

Mithraism was influential enough to leave Mithraic temples wherever Imperial Rome stationed substantial garrisons. Mithraists had a complex system of hierarchical ranks. Mithraic and military rank went hand in hand – it may be considered analogous, if not a likely forerunner, to being a Freemason in modern business circles.

It is tempting to dismiss Mithraism as a dumbed-down version of Zoroastrianism, reduced to an idol cult with only vague references to the original creed (for instance, that of the sun being the embodiment of the Creator). It may have been possible to write off Mithraic legacy if we knew more about it, but we do not – its followers knew how to keep secrets.

The exclusively military membership may have accelerated its demise during the collapse of

Western Rome: it may have even been amalgamated with Christianity by order of its leadership. At any rate, Mithraism was never a serious opponent for emerging Christianity. Following the prohibition of idolatry in the fifth century, all references to it cease.

There is some irony in the fact that the Roman military followed a religion borrowed from their worst enemy – but since wars with Carthage the Romans excelled in borrowing successful strategies, tools and concepts from their enemies. Iran was the only such enemy not be defeated in due course, and it made sense that Roman soldiers felt a compulsion to try out Iranian ways.

One is reminded of Goebbles, who forced the hapless SS troopers to breakfast on porridge. It was, he declared, the food of British Empire builders, and the builders of the nascent Reich had to take the same medicine.

In summary, the first millennium may be viewed from the following perspective. Two superpowers, Rome and Iran, were locked in a border war that spanned generations, technologies and dynasties. Neither empire was fighting for survival, but the conflict was key to the movement of many resources, not to mention national prestige.

But military action is only the more visible part

of this conflict. There was also a war of creeds, with each empire adopting a different national religion – a practice new to the science of empire building. Both sides now used religion as a tool of imperial governance as well as a shibboleth of good citizenship – and that was very new.

Zoroastrians formulated this approach approximately a century before the Romans. When the church of Rome still struggled against state persecution, the Zoroastrian church was an essential element in power politics as well as a government-sponsored arbiter of social mores.

As it evolved in the shadow of ongoing conflict between Rome and Iran, Christianity was able to save itself a lot of trial and error by borrowing from the established model of state religion in Iran.

Above: A bas-relief showing the first Sassanian king, Ardashir I as blessed by Ahura Mazda (leftmost horseman). Below: Coins bearing images of Sassanid emperors.

The image of Shapur II. Elegantly crafted artworks of this nature were mass-produced and distributed in the Sassanian times as state propaganda.

Remains of a palace at Ctesiphon (believed to be built by Khosroes I), photographed in 1921. The city was destroyed by Arab armies in 637.

Further evolution of dualist thought

Another famous dualist offshoot was Manicheism, which had sprouted much deeper roots in the West than Mithraism.

According to some, that dark, unworldly import is still with us. It certainly made a lot of news until the twelfth century when Cathars, its last known descendants, met their end in the blood-soaked orgy, known as the Albigensian Crusade.

Mani built his religion on the platform of dualist eschatology, teaching that the spiritual world was created by God, and the physical, corruptible world was in turn made by Satan. He identified denial of the physical world as the only path to salvation.

The second strand to the Manichean doctrine was gnosticism – a line of thought that swirled around the Greek world for some time. Gnosticism is worth understanding to assess the direction of religious history and the cross-roads it faced in the third and fourth century AD.

In simple essence, gnosticism ("knowledge") consists of the concept that worship should consist of an abstract, spiritual communion with the divine rather than concrete actions such as formal prayers or sacrifices. Developed a little further, this line of thought suggests that the rational mind cannot be wrapped around the concept of the divine. This is the crux of the "knowledge" - that rational process can play no meaningful part in worship.

There was a good reason for evolution of this philosophy in the Greek world, whose intellectual tradition has never been reconciled with the traditional Olympic pantheon. The classic gods of Homer provided the Greeks with plenty of amusing and poignant folklore, but these flawed, corrupt and capricious anthropomorphisms were not at all about to yield answers to profound cosmological and ethical questions.

That created a powerful vacuum, which the so-called Neo-Platonists were not slow to fill. Their school of pagan gnosticism put the individual pagan gods into what photographers euphemistically call soft focus. This was considered a serious challenge to fledgling Christianity, as evidenced by the carefully preserved works by early church fathers who counter the Neo-Platonist arguments and polemic.

Mani grew up in Babylon, which exposed him to all strands of religious innovation unleashed on the ancient world in that era – Christianity of the Romans to the west, Zoroastrian (Zurvanist) Iran to the east and the Greek Neo-Platonism to the north. Later in his life he journeyed to the southern reaches of the Sassanid territory, where he encountered Buddhism – after which he added the doctrine of reincarnation to his brew.

Mani's activities could be summarized as copying the most appealing elements from every religion he encountered. That may sound as if he was a lightweight challenger to Christianity and Zoroastrianism, but facts state otherwise. Manicheism became highly popular and influential, especially after Mani's death.

He was eventually executed at the behest of the Zoroastrian establishment (either crucified, flayed or beheaded, according to varying traditions), but Manicheism had jumped the frontier, igniting a much larger following on the Roman side.

To appreciate its appeal, one has to return to the perspective in fourth century AD: two powerful and rival states, each with its own state religion – and an ecclesiastic apparatus that relied on secular power to suppress heresy. Disagreement with official dogma was no mere religious dispute, but treason against the state.

Manicheism challenged official religions on both sides of the frontier. It radically differed from official Christianity, especially over the mechanism of redemption, and it rejected the fundamental tenet of Zoroastrianism – that worship of Ahura-Mazda consists of adhering to a moral system, and subscription to that moral system requires a constant effort.

Manicheism shifted the emphasis – away from real-world goals of a moral creed and towards the Buddhist ideal – withdrawal from the material world in pursuit of a spiritual union with the Godhead.

The evident appeal of this philosophy to those leading complex lives in an increasingly cramped world is self-evident to a modern observer, and it would have been at least as clear to the citizens of the increasingly contradictory reality of Zurvanist Iran – a wealthy and advanced society, suffering increasing corruption, despotism and constant war, all cutting across the fundamental tenets of Zarathustra. Likewise, the brutally violent Realpolitik of Imperial Rome, whose restraint of free trade saw a rapid deterioration in its economic circumstances, presented a powerful temptation to withdraw from reality.

That appeal is well-documented by a former Manichean who became one of the most influential Christian thinkers – Augustine of Hippo, better known as St Augustine. He admitted that in comparison with Orthodox Christianity, Mani's creed was seduction itself. It offered a path to salvation without the handicap of original sin. Redemption lay in making a spiritual effort, rather than abject submission central to Catholicism.

That distinction is crucial, for the Roman Empire contained two ideological strands. One was the original heritage of early Roman republic – an iron-fisted state, whose citizens obey the law in spirit as well as in letter, with utter contempt for the well-being of themselves or others whenever state business was transacted.

The old Roman was primarily a soldier. He viewed his civilian responsibilities – a governor of his family and a careful gatherer of economic wealth – with the same *gravitas* as his military duty to die for his country. He was suspicious of material pleasures and despised anything that did not involve war or productivity.

In the heady days of Imperial Rome that mindset began to be displaced by a more free-wheeling model, consisting, broadly, of "smelling the roses", as befits the rightful citizen of a global empire, whose peak living standards and economic wealth were not reconstructed until the nineteenth century.

The new Roman was a hedonist profoundly immersed in the pursuit of pleasure. He felt increasingly unhappy about donning armour and sleeping in frozen mud at a barely known corner of his vast empire. He was spiritually divorced from being a cog in a war machine that built his nation – with the obvious contribution towards its weakening. In addition, from second century AD onwards, that nouveau Roman was increasingly likely to be of non-Roman heritage, exposed to at least one other culture from birth.

To illustrate the cultural complexity of that time, one needs to consider that Jesus and His followers were trilingual – in daily life they spoke Aramaic (a Semitic language related to Hebrew, widely used throughout Mesopotamia), read scriptures in Hebrew, plus Greek that was the main language of commerce and the language of the colonial Roman administration.

That was no mere knowledge of languages either – most subjects of the Caesars lived astride at least two different cultures, each with a distinct heritage, ethical system and religious profile. Christianity and Manicheism fought for followers in a very open market. Both religions adopted Jesus, albeit in very different forms. The vehemence, with which the early church fathers denounced Manicheism, indicates that the latter was a credible competitor in that marketplace.

Eventually the Roman strand prevailed. Its simple requirement – that a convert signed on the dotted line and followed orders thereafter – proved to have greater mass appeal than the complex gnostic weave of Mani, whose Zurvanist-derived cosmology with one primary deity creating another was even harder to process that the Trinity of the Christians, who spent an entire century fighting over whether the living Jesus was physical or divine.

The victory of Christianity was aided by the fact that times were rapidly changing. Roman economic and military power had suffered a rapid erosion, and living standards plummeted with every generation from third century onwards. The era of sophisticated hedonists who could afford to drop out of reality had run its course.

Manicheans were first reviled, then suppressed and finally hunted out of existence in Western Europe. It is most likely that underground communities remained – the ensuing five centuries saw great disorder and total loss of central control. Most Europeans who lived after the collapse of Western Rome were preoccupied with survival in the face of frequent war and a food supply much diminished because of technological regression. The remnant of central government that remained was fully preoccupied with survival as an organized power. Whatever power it commanded was fighting a rearguard action against the hordes of hungry and well-armed migrants, whose movements made the political map of Europe change like a lava lamp. No government had the means to engage in religious repression en masse.

In the seventh century the Arabs appeared on Europe's doorstep. They occupied modern Portugal and Spain, then crossed the Pyrenees to establish several strongholds in modern France.

Besieged by such a deadly threat, Catholic Europe was not in a position to orchestrate a systematic assault on heresy. This was the case until the thirteenth century, when Europeans were numerous enough and wealthy enough to divert enough resources from its battle with Islam to hurl a separate crusade against fellow Christians.

That crusade targeted the Cathars, a secretive dualistic sect. Cathars believed that the divine spirit within humanity had become imprisoned by corruption that was inextricable from the material world.

The only detailed information about Cathars comes from their sworn enemies, such as the Inquisition, which was quick to accuse all heretics of devil worship. Allowing for that distortion, it still appears Cathars considered the world as created by Satan, whom they considered a supernatural along Zoroastrian lines – one not to be worshipped. The difference was that combat against evil was considered to be a purely spiritual affair. Violence was not the Cathar way, which may be considered a major ideological failing at that time. The Cathar ideal was that of an unworldly ascetic, rather than a warrior on constant standby.

Furthermore, it is said that Cathars considered the God worshipped by most Christians as an imposter, and the church who worshipped Him was corrupt as a consequence (the corruption of the papal establishment being self-evident at that point).

The aim of any Cathar was to become free of the material realm. The means to do so lay through understanding the corrupt and limited nature of material existence and the artifice of religious practices, imposed by the state religion.

The lure of Cathars' religion is self-evident once the observer visualizes their world. At the beginning of the second millennium AD Europe was a miserable cocktail of sleet, war and famine. A religion that allowed one to treat that reality with disdain was a useful adaptation device, and the orthodox church did its utmost to promise a better world in heaven. Cathars did one better – they suggested that there is a way to make the suffering of this world insubstantial and irrelevant to one's well-being.

The Cathar ideal was a quasi-monastic state of the *Parfaits* ("the perfect ones"), as opposed to the lay adherents, who were known as *Credentes* ("the believers"). The Parfaits may be described as living ideals of earthly existence – bereft of any material possessions, living off non-animal matter and devoted purely to tending to the flock – teaching, praying, preaching and performing the sometimes appalling duties left to monastic institutions in that era, such as tending to the dying. Sex was considered the realm of Satan himself, even in marriage, which was also considered a necessary evil.

Other Cathars were supposed to do their best to emulate the *Parfait* ideals. In addition, they were forbidden to perpetrate violence and swear oaths, which essentially excluded them from contemporary commerce.

There are many close parallels between the stratification of Cathar community and that of Manicheans, who were headed by the ascetic elite, essentially the upper echelon of the clergy required to abstain from most material pleasures. The lower rank consisted of those with a lesser restriction on their lifestyle, and at the bottom of the pyramid was the bulk of the population who enjoyed no restriction on their pleasures.

In matters of doctrine, the Cathars rejected many parts of the New Testament and all of the Hebrew Bible, which they believed to have been inspired by Satan. Jesus was considered a purely spiritual manifestation of God, but His divinity was otherwise entirely denied. They also appeared not to believe in hell, instead believing in reincarnation. They considered this world as hell itself; a return to it after reincarnation was viewed with the same terror as the prospect of ending up in hell for traditional Catholics.

One can see how Cathars made themselves unpopular in papal Europe. Apart from flatly contradicting many a dogma of the ruling establishment, they harshly denounced the wealth to which the church hierarchy had become much accustomed.

The origin of Cathars is entirely lost to history. What may be said reasonably is that their first appearance is dated just after the era of Bogomils. Given the similarity of their creeds, it is reasonable to suggest that one was at least partially related to the other genetically.

Bogomils ("beloved by God", alternatively "admirers of God") were another dualist sect. They originated in Bulgaria, then an independent Slavic kingdom. Being only loosely governed by warlords, Bulgarians enjoyed religious freedom quite beyond the reach of either ruling church, living in the geographic watershed between the Catholic Western Europe and the Orthodox Byzantium.

Bogomil preachers travelled extensively in Europe. They always did so in pairs and were exclusively male. Their mainstream opponents were not slow to notice this fact and to start a rumour (possibly true but a common slander for that time, especially where heretics were concerned) that they were homosexuals. The were known as Bulgars, or Bougrres in French, and this is believed to be the origin of the term "bugger".

Like most sects opposed to mainstream Christianity, Bogomils were avowed Gnostics, whose appeal was especially great in the era of deepening religious disputation. The mainstream Church and European society at large were increasingly bogged down in idiotic debates, at the expense of urgent real-world problems such as rapid loss of formerly Roman territory. Political exploitation of theological squabbles eventually resulted in a disastrous schism between the Roman West and the Byzantine East, a splitting of the Christian world that eventually resulted in the greatest loss of Christian territory to Islam.

In all likelihood, those who responded to Bogomil teachings eventually coalesced with the Cathars, who were a prominent population in the south of modern France, then Languedoc ("Langue d'Oc" meaning Language of Occitan, a Romance language related to French). They were also present in relatively large numbers in the mountains of Northern Italy and Spain.

There are various explanations for this geographic distribution. It may have something to do with an Iranian tribe of Alans, presumably dualists and possibly Manicheans, who settled in Southern France around the sixth century. There is a more obvious reason – mountains offer a very realistic advantage in defensive wars, especially if one is outnumbered by the likely enemy. Mountain roads can be defended with few troops, being easily rendered impassable or blocked by fire from overlooking castles. Armies crossing the mountains must allow for a lot of extra time and resources, and movement is slow. Food is easily denied to an invader – those who made the crossing had to carry whatever they intended to eat en route. In addition, the time it took to complete the crossing was entirely at the mercy of the weather, something that changes every few hours in the mountains. At best, an army crossing the mountains could not hope to surprise their inhabitants as it was unable to move at speed. Finally, campaigns were unlikely to enjoy any form of success outside a few brief months of alpine summer.

Cathars were not the only religious minority who made their home in the mountains for these reasons. Assassins, a mediaeval Islamic sect reviled by other Muslims and the Druze, whose religion is a departure from Islam, also sought the mountains for shelter from the keepers of official dogma.

Mounted during the twelfth century, the Albigensian Crusade (Albi being a town in Southern France, roughly the geographic centre of the Cathar population), represented a colossal misappropriation of manpower from the battle against Islam, which was by then at full swing.

Crusaders devastated southern France and killed

a large number of local inhabitants. Because it was impossible to pick Cathars from observant Catholics (who were permitted by their faith to masquerade as orthodox Christians), the crusaders adopted the now famous "Kill them all, God will recognize his own" strategy. (Allegedly, that was the statement of the papal legate verbatim, when the Catholic general baulked at setting fire to a cathedral with some thousand local inhabitants trapped inside).

The outcome was a fiery cautery of Cathar heresy, some followers of which resisted in their mountain strongholds for many years. It was a total success – never again was there a significant dualist presence on European soil.

Apart from leaving Southern France with a demographics shift present even today, the campaign also marked the high point in the political ascendancy of papacy. The same crusade gave new prominence to the fledgling Inquisition and turned it into an instrument of truly Gothic terror for centuries to come (Spain was the last jurisdiction where the Inquisition was active in 1809, officially abolished by Napoleon after the conquest of Spain).

It is said that the Cathar movement, far from disappearing, has become one of the drivers of Reformation. That seems a long bow to draw, since the thrust of the Protestant doctrine is even further from Cathar principles than that of

Catholicism, and survival in any numbers for three hundred years – under the rabid gaze of the Inquisition – is unlikely anywhere in Catholic Europe.

It would therefore appear that Manicheanism was destroyed in the twelfth century, at best leaving small cells of secret worshippers. If they survived long enough to contribute to the bubbling cauldron of Reformation, their contribution would have been in the form of general resentment for the rich papal establishment, possibly as local muscle, rather than significant contributors to the Protestant creed. Besides, any surviving memory of Cathars was likely to be tainted with odious labels of sodomy and Satan worship.

It may therefore be concluded that the dualist influence ceased to be exerted on the Christian world after the Albigensian Crusade. The Indo-European method of resolving disputes has demonstrated its effectiveness yet again.

What about Islam?

Not strictly the subject of this book, the interactions between Zoroastrianism and Islam are worth a few additional points.

Islam was heavily influenced by Zoroastrianism at inception, directly as well as through Jewish and Christian sources. But it is difficult to see how Zoroastrian thoughts could get through the door ever since.

The rise of Islam from its singular source is meticulously documented, unlike the evolution of early Christianity. There is no evidence of Islam changing significantly as a result of exposure to external ideas. As many of its critics point out, therein lies the problem.

There are many branches and genetic descendants of Islam that may be better viewed as breakaway sects: the Ismailis, the Assassins and the Druze. All of these originated a number of centuries after the fall of Iran. At the time of their origin Zoroastrians were a persecuted minority scattered and even hidden on the territory once occupied by Sassanid Iran. During Middle Ages Iranian Zoroastrians survived only as hated and heavily oppressed subjects of an Islamic order. The one visible community of Zoroastrian immigrants, the Parsees, enjoyed little more than tolerance by the Islamic rulers of Gujarat. There is little to support an assertion that any of these made an impact on Islamic doctrine of their conquerors.

The Baha'i religion, whose origin is very recent (reputedly, nineteenth century), combines the elements of Judaism, Christianity and Islam, but also accords a special place to Zoroaster as the forerunner of these religions.

The Shia branch of Islam may have inherited subliminal influences of Zoroastrianism since the vast majority of Shiites live on the territories of the former Sassanid Empire, but a more learned man will have to discern such threads. There is no Islamic equivalent of the Cathar movement with a strong tradition of dualism – any suggestion that God is not omniscient and omnipotent would mortally offend orthodox Muslims.

Any search for Zoroastrian influence on Islamic doctrine has to be distinguished from the obvious relationship between Islamic and Iranian civilizations. Much of what we associate with the Orient has originated in Iran, and the Arabs eagerly adopted all of it. It does not, however, appear that any of it came from the contemporary Iranian religion. That is not altogether surprising; by the time of the Iranian conquest the compilation of the Koran was well and truly over, and the time window for further syncretism was well and truly closed.

Playing the devil's advocate, it is not difficult to envisage that conquering Arabs saw Sassanid Zoroastrians as idolaters not at all worthy of emulation – because what they encountered was not the "clean" fundamentalist Zoroastrianism but its Zurvanist variant.

That is why any religious influence by the conquered and persecuted Zoroastrians was necessarily minor. It would be surprising if it were otherwise – just as exposure to Jewish communities all over Europe did nothing to advance the evolution of Christianity, until Reformation made it possible to reach back to the Judaic roots of a thoroughly Europeanized religion.

Islam never had a Reformation. It remains a seventh century creed, and many things that were workable then are no longer workable today.

Whilst Arabs also adopted from Christian Byzantium, whose territories they conquered even before they got to Iran, there is no question that they ceased to be galloping desert nomads and became a dazzling civilization precisely when they became the masters of Iran.

The Sassanid decline

In late Sassanid era things got even stranger after Mani. Another dualist innovator called Mazdak is accorded the dubious honour of becoming the world's first practising communist in the Maoist mould. One may object that the first communists in history were the Pythagorean sect, mimicked by Essenes in Judea who authored the Dead Sea Scrolls – but neither of these advocated their communal way of life for the society at large.

Mazdak preached abolition of rights to private property, especially land. He even extended this theory to sharing spouses. His views were initially adopted by an enthusiastic ruler, who even began to implement the first Communist society in history against, not surprisingly, resistance from saner citizens.

The brief rule of Mazdakism ended in civil war, and the convert-king was eventually killed by his traditionalist son, who went on to slaughter Mazdak and his supporters.

Christians and Jews fell in and out of favour during the Sassanid centuries. In Iran Christians were always distrusted because of the Roman connection. Nestorian Christians were officially welcomed because Nestorians, who were persecuted in Rome, chose to move to the east of the frontier. It was entirely accidental that Nestor, the founder of the doctrine, received most of his support from the provinces bordering Iran, and the Iranians encouraged them and granted Nestorians protection on the divide-and-rule principle in their constant battle with Byzantium. The Nestorians believed that Jesus was two separate persons – the physical and the divine being who dwelt in the physical. There was no other aspect of their dogma that would have made them more acceptable to Zoroastrianism.

The Jews, traditional allies of the Iranians in creed and in resentment of pagan hegemony, also enjoyed uneven progress, as illustrated by their occasional privileged legal status under some Sassanid kings – Shapur I had a lifelong friendship with Shmuel, the leader of the Babylonian Jewish community; also Shapur II and Bahram V were born of Jewish mothers. Yet later Jews faced persecution under Yezdegerd II, sufficient to force them to flee to the neighbouring domain of Khozars. Despite the friendship between Shapur I and Shmuel, there were repressive laws against Jews that Shmuel succeeded in repealing, indicating that all was never well.

The fate of Jews in Zoroastrian Iran is a fascinating laboratory for students of anti-Semitism. Jews were widely reviled in the Greek world, almost certainly as a result of their identification (by Greeks) with their close relatives, the hated Phoenicians. The latter, until annihilated by Rome, kept the Greeks out of Western Mediterranean for nearly a thousand years. Greek anti-Semitism is very evident in the Gospel of Luke, a Syriac of Greek background. The venom expended on Jews by early Christian ideologues of Greek origin, well exemplified in the rantings of Eusebius and John Chrysostom ("golden mouth") clearly pre-dates (and contradicts) Christianity.

Romans were well-disposed towards Jews, despite the fundamentalist-led revolts that eventually resulted in the destruction of Judea. Most of the Jews enslaved during Judean wars were freed within a generation, to join the large and wealthy community in Rome. Tiberius even passed laws allowing Jews to observe Sabbath, where this clashed with various demands made on traders by Roman law.

Throughout the ages, Christians and Muslims have behaved variously towards Jews, ranging from officially sanctioned pogroms to benevolence that allowed Jews to flourish. However, this took place in the shadow of deeply anti-Semitic content of their holy books (Mohammed turned on Jews for rejecting his creed much like Martin Luther, who was equally enraged by their refusal to be absorbed into what he considered a return to Judaic roots).

Now, Zoroastrian Iran had no anti-Semitic antecedents in its religion or politics. From Cyrus onwards, Jews and Iranians were always on the same side. Jews borrowed such a large amount of Zoroastrian doctrine that their faith after that point could be viewed as a variant of Zoroastrianism by a casual observer.

Even the very term "Pharisee" may not have come from the Hebrew *perushim* – "the separate ones". Why did that name stick, when Pharisees were the majority? A more likely derivation is *Parsim* ("Persian"), referring to the post-Temple doctrine of Judaism that developed in Babylonian exile under Persian rule – in the same manner as European Jews are called Ashkenazim – a geographic term that also reflects a different interpretation of Judaism (*Ashkenaz* is a Middle Hebrew term for the area roughly corresponding to modern Germany).

The Jewish purity laws, which made them appear so aloof and bizarre to Gentiles, were almost identical to those of Zoroastrians. Their codes of personal conduct and sexual modesty, a source of much derision in the pagan world, were eminently recognizable to any Zoroastrian.

Nevertheless, Jews encountered persecution in Sassanid Iran. The precise circumstances leading to this are lost to history, but one may guess that Iranians were as human as anyone else when it comes to xenophobia and jealousy over a minority's economic success. The rather ironic anti-Semitism of Abrahamic religions does not appear to be unique.

These are sadly familiar traits, splinter movements and violent persecutions of religions and sects that fall in and out of favour. But they should be no surprise to any student of Christian or Islamic history, who will be aware that a religion becomes morally confused and engages in violence almost as a matter of course once, it becomes part of a government apparatus.

We may surmise that similar developments were observed in Zoroastrian Iran. Had Arabs not put an end to Zoroastrianism as an official religion of a muscular state, it would eventually follow a similar political trajectory to Catholicism – a blood-soaked excursion into geopolitics and totalitarianism.

Centuries of being a religion of a minority, sometimes left alone but more often persecuted and harassed, makes a creed compete for survival, forcing it to become more relevant to the needs of its believers.

It may be suggested that Zoroastrianism preserved its good name by being dethroned, before too many reprehensible actions were perpetrated in its name. Like Judaism and Protestant Christianity, it was forced to return to its grass roots. For many centuries it was a religion of a persecuted minority: being a Zoroastrian offered no political or economic advantage.

The benefits of being a member of a close-knit community were more than offset by the hostility of local authorities. One does not get further in society by being a Zoroastrian or a Jew. Contrary to what business competitors may whisper about minority groups, one would be entirely better off to assume the identity of the ruling majority.

Nevertheless, those religions had survived – because, runs the inescapable conclusion, they offer a positive contribution to survival of their followers.

Much derision is levelled at Iran because it collapsed under the Arab attack when its rival Indo-European culture of the West has survived. It may be tempting to dismiss Zoroastrian Iran on that basis, but a more comprehensive analysis offers a different perspective.

Christians lost a vast amount of territory to the Arabs over the first three centuries of Arab expansion – nearly all the conquests apart from Iran were Christian territory. It is difficult to fathom today that the Middle East and North Africa were Christian for nearly four hundred years when conquered by Arabs. Very little of that legacy remained four centuries later when Christians reconquered a small patch of territory in the Middle East.

The Arab invasion of Europe was stopped on two

fronts: in the south of modern Russia, by nomadic Khozars, a fascinating historic anomaly of a Turkic tribe that converted to Judaism. They used similar military tactics to Mongols – a blitzkrieg on horseback, devastating the enemy with arrows fired from full gallop. The Arab armies had no answer to these tactics, as their encounters with Mongols demonstrated later.

On the second front, celebrated in European folklore, a trans-Pyrenean invasion was mounted from Spain, by that stage already an Arab province. It was stopped by the Franks, led by Charles Martel, in 732. That encounter broke the back of subsequent attempts by Spanish Muslims to cross into France, although it took another seven centuries to evict the Arabs from European territories of modern Spain and Portugal.

The Pyrenees proved a formidable barrier. Whilst it would be presumptive to suggest that Arab armies could not adapt to European conditions – they did so in Spain – crossing the mountains in numbers was a seasonal activity that could not be repeated with ease, and an army weakened by a mountain crossing was confronted by a freshly rested force on arrival.

There were no savage horsemen or tall mountains to protect Iran. Its Zagros range is easily bypassed from both north and south. The Caucasian mountains proved more of an obstacle – hence the survival of Iranian cultures of

Ossetia, Armenia and Georgia, despite eventual conversion to Christianity and Islam.

But the Zoroastrian hinterland was sited in the indefensible lowlands of Central Asia. There was no expendable buffer zone like Spain and no distant colonies or provinces to fall back on – unlike Christianity, whose outlying areas alone took the Arabs two centuries to conquer. The territory that contained all of the world's Zoroastrians was well within the reach of Arab armies and their supply lines.

The flat land of Central Asia was ideally suited to Arab military tactics, and it fell in a few short decades. Western Europe, even if the Pyrenees were not a barrier, was broken country and largely forested at the time. The Mongol experience in Russia showed that mounted armies are useless in this terrain: Northern Russia, largely covered by forest during the Mongol invasion, remained untouched. The Mongols could only move over frozen rivers in winter, attacking riverside settlements. But they could not follow those who fled into the forest.

European terrain favours the infantry, a much cheaper kind of military force to field. A helmet, a pike, an axe and a wooden shield cost a fraction of a horseman's armour. Such equipment could be fashioned by any village blacksmith, whereas a suit of armour that permits full movement required rare expertise. Training an infantry force requires only a few weeks, even today – whereas the making of an armoured knight is a lifelong commitment.

Sassanid legacy

Right up to the time of its destruction, the Sassanid society was a powerful, viable empire that continued to expand at the expense of its Byzantine neighbour.

Its abrupt demise ended 1,100 years of Zoroastrian order, an era that left an enormous legacy. Little of it is attributed to its true origin now – mainly because much of that legacy has since been plagiarized. The inheritors of such plagiarism had the power and the motives to erase the memory of original authors, in order to hide the plagiarism.

The Sassanid Empire continued to flex its military muscle, slowly restoring former Achaemenid territory to Iranian control. It did not enjoy ubiquitous success but progress was steady. It is little known today that Iranians took back Jerusalem only a few decades before the Arab conquest. Clearly, the Zurvanist priesthood was not much of an impediment.

The rituals of the Iranian court were already ancient, institutionalized at the time of Cyrus and retained even under the Greeks by the satraps. The Greeks, starting famously with Alexander himself, imitated the Iranian ways, which implied that the king was an absolute master. Indeed, it was Alexander's decree that all his war companions must now approach him on their knees that cost the life of one of his closest associates (after which Alexander repented).

The same Persian rituals were later imported into barbarian Europe verbatim. Most familiar conventions of running a feudal kingdom from the monarch's palace are Iranian. There was simply no one else to imitate – Rome was simply too new to the business of running dynastic empires, and none of its enemies, apart from the Iranians, deserved imitation.

Life in everyday Iran of the first millennium, alas, remains something of a guess reconstructed from scarce artefacts from that era. The main reason for this paucity of information stems from the cultural and physical holocaust that took place after Islamic invasion.

Even bloody-minded invaders inadvertently leave plentiful numerous of a conquered culture – half-heartedly defaced inscriptions, scorched documents and broken works of art are left in the rubble of destroyed cities and the original purpose of surviving buildings is not difficult to discern in converted temples and palaces.

Not so in Iran, where many such artefacts appear to have undergone systematic erasure. Iranian culture lacked the good fortune of the Romans, whose civilization remained functional in the east when it was trampled into mud in the West. In Europe books were snatched out of the path of rampaging armies into the safety of monasteries, where preservation was ensured, albeit with considerable censorship. Nothing like that occurred in the Zoroastrian world, which succumbed and vanished within a few generations, leaving a few residual communities as islands in a hostile Moslem sea.

The full impact of Sassanid splendour on the world culture will probably never be known. We will continue to take for granted its achievements, such as the code of chivalry and the feudal system, or customs, such as shaking hands and playing chess.

Others, such as Arabs and Europeans have done an excellent job of claiming these advances as their own.

As they say in Russia, there is no law that mandates the world to be fair.

Zoroastrianism today

The creed of Zarathushtra is still practised by around half a million followers who reside in Iran, plus small Indian community of Parsees, whose ancestors escaped to India during the mediaeval period. Zoroastrians were never proselytizers; indeed one cannot, strictly speaking, convert to Zoroastrianism – a problem now hotly debated by leaders of Zoroastrian communities in the melting pots in Europe, USA and other multicultural societies, where many Zoroastrians find themselves today.

It is not surprising that they throve as an exiled minority in India and thrive now elsewhere. They have a reputation for scrupulous honesty in business and a strong sense of community – but this is not a testament to superiority of their religion. Many ethnic communities succeed in exile – Orthodox Jews, Christian Armenians, Chinese Buddhists and Muslim Lebanese. One cannot attribute their success to a religion.

The modern faith is very close to the spirit of original Zoroastrian fundamentalism. The most important difference appears to be a watering down of the militaristic aspect of Zoroastrian dualism. This is understandable, given that modern Zoroastrians are descendants of barely tolerated minorities, surviving and being able to practise their religion entirely at the pleasure of the authorities.

Like trendy modern Christian theologians, the Parsees had watered down their Satan to a manifestation of human psyche, rather than an abstract force dedicated to undoing of the Creation. It is a significant step away from the doctrine of absolute personal responsibility and one designed to give more room for the collectivism of the "I was only following orders" variety. One cannot help but think that this is not what Zarathushtra had in mind.

Parsee communities, much like those of remaining Zoroastrians in Iran, remain discrete and obscure. They engage in a vast amount of charitable works, but they do not advertise, display or proselytize. Zoroastrian voices are very seldom heard in a modern debate. Few successful Zoroastrians (who are many) even identify their heritage to outsiders.

Parsee rituals preserve religious customs their ancestors took from Iran. Their lifestyle emphasizes cleanliness, decency and hard work.

The Zoroastrian equivalent of confirmation is performed at fifteenth birthday, the age that ancient Iranians considered the mark of maturation. Parsees wear a traditional belt, a *kusti,* underneath their clothing. It is made of two ropes, tied with two knots, one at the front and one at the back, and it symbolizes the mark of voluntary adherence to the faith. Zoroastrians say five brief prayers per day and worship in temples, where a sacred flame is maintained by a *mobed*, a close equivalent of a parish priest.

Zoroastrians tend to worship in discrete seclusion from the rest of society and prefer to marry their own. Until the advent of the Internet they were hard to find outside their traditional enclaves. They do not encourage inquiries, seek no converts and marry mainly within their own communities. The latter practice is contributing to a severe drop in their numbers, and it is difficult to comprehend.

The Jews, traditionally prohibited from marrying non-Jews, have evolved many pathways that allow conversion and a religiously sanctioned union, whose offspring are recognized as Jews. The amount of common sense that is applied in the process of conversion varies between congregations, but it is possible, without too much anguish, for a moderately orthodox Jew to marry a converted partner in a liberal temple. A testament to the success of this process is confirmed by modern genetics, which suggests that the male genes of modern Jews still carry evidence of a distinct Semitic origin, but the DNA of mitochondria, cell components only transmitted by the mother, show a much broader ethnic mix.

Orthodox Zoroastrians do not acknowledge any conversion rituals, and a number of times this issue has come before Indian courts. In its most severe form, Parsee Zoroastrianism does not recognize the offspring of a mixed marriage; a Zoroastrian is defined as someone of either Parsee descent or coming from a surviving Iranian communities.

In the past forty years Parsees have migrated to other countries in large numbers, and these communities have necessarily adopted a more liberal stance towards conversion. There is, reportedly, a steady rise in the numbers, due to conversion by escapees from that most prevalent of modern religions, consumption in a moral vacuum. If so, Zoroastrianism is the oldest religion set to experience a revival.

Zoroastrian antecedents in the political culture of modern West

England was a latecomer to the social and political cataclysm of Reformation. A good century since Henry VIII declared Rome and its religion corrupt manifestations of foreign power, the resentment against the old power elite organized from the Vatican, has crystallized as the English Puritan movement – a political, ethical and aesthetic antithesis of everything the Catholic establishment signified and stood for.

The English Civil War was a product of that cleavage. A king foolish enough to accentuate and exacerbate that social divide has paid for his error with his head. The execution of Charles I, if not entirely deserved or lawful, was a minor loss to British society. But it caused a sensation at the time, becoming a fulcrum for a profound remodelling of English society.

After installation of Puritan Cromwell as a dictator, in the original Roman sense of the word, Puritan ideology became a bona fide alternative to the established culture grouped around "high church" Anglicanism, still feudal Catholicism in all but name.

The Puritans ran England but briefly, yet many of her essential institutions were founded during that short period. Puritan reforms laid what are now regarded as cornerstones of not only modern England, but every developed society since – no one can deny the geopolitical achievements of English-speaking nations.

Puritans took their values to North American colonies. Today they are celebrated as the ongoing source of American prosperity.

Like all Protestants, the Puritans derived their basic aspirations from the Old Testament. They treated the New Testament with suspicion, precisely because it bears the obvious marks of revisionism, which make the entire document look quite bereft of divine inspiration.

The English Puritans found themselves to be very similar to contemporary Jews in outlook, behaviour and success. To this day, only English-speaking Christians bear names like Moses, David or Israel. In countries like France, Germany or Russia anyone called Isaac or Sarah can be instantly identified as a Jew.

It is not surprising that English-speaking world has proved to be the most welcoming environment that Jews have ever known in exile. It has been so for four centuries, and the relationship shows no sign of withering.

One of the most important qualities that distinguishes post-Puritan Englishmen from German or Russian contemporaries may be described as a dogmatic and self-fulfilling optimism. "Never say die" built one of the greatest empires in history, and even after its eclipse in the formal sense, Anglo-Saxons remain the self-appointed policemen of the globe, not to mention majority shareholders in its economic wealth.

The source of such inspiration should be instantly familiar to the reader of these pages. It is Zarathushtra's world view – success comes of toil, honesty and persistence, violence being viewed with distaste, yet vigorously practised whenever required. That view was distilled from the Persian-inspired revision of the Jewish tradition, written down as the Old Testament.

It is worth pausing to note what the Hebrew Bible comprises. Once a collection of oral and written sagas of a militant semi-nomadic people, it was committed to parchment shortly after of the Babylonian Exile. At the same time Judaism has undergone a change, assuming its modern form.

The impetus to both events was contact with Persians, whose success and breadth of religious vision the Jews found to their liking. Their vision stayed with the Jews since, and it is they who handed it on to Romans and their European successors.

Early Roman Christianity found itself in possession of a number of Jewish principles which they could not hope to sell to either the

Roman establishment or the Roman mob. It altered the emphasis of their creed to suit the new political requirements, burying the Persian legacy of the Hebrew Bible under debates over whether Jesus was man or spirit, two entities or one, son of God by direct insemination of a mortal woman or a divine spirit manifesting as a man.

These debates were further spiced by incineration of heretics and papal corruption. By the time of Reformation the doctrine of the Western church was bogged in self-indulgent nonsense – at best the Catholic Church failed to assist the evolution of the society it ruled. Even today we see Catholicism tear itself in senseless struggles with medical technology and new ethical dilemmas. Many Catholics depart – first the Sunday mass, then God, over issues such as contraception and sexual practices. Many lapsed Catholics find it all too easy to discard everything associated with religion, including the basics of morality.

The Roman shroud, in which Christianity was tightly wrapped, was somewhat loosened during Reformation. Underneath that tattered cloth the Protestant rebels found a very different religion with an unfamiliar ethos. History testifies that the result was an explosion in productivity and wealth, not to mention rapid shifts in the balance of global power. Zarathushtra would have admired the successful husbandry of the

Protestant world.

The impetus to finalize the Hebrew Bible began when Jews exiled to Babylon discovered that they are not going to be massacred, worked to death or sacrificed to heathen idols. Far from having to break rocks in chains, they soon became wealthy citizens of the conquering nation.

Whilst Jews may have wept for Zion by the rivers of Babylon, their identity did not appear to be under any kind of violent threat. In fact, the new circumstances presented an opposite danger – it was all too easy to assimilate. The definition and preservation of Jewish identity suddenly became an issue of unprecedented priority.

Shortly after he took Babylon, Cyrus ordered the entire Zoroastrian tradition to be written down, and this process would have served as a template for the Jews. It was also the best opportunity for finalizing the contents of the holy library. The military annihilation of Judah, its population exiled in chains, has culled many rival factions and scholars. In all likelihood, the more fanatical and the less reasonable of these rivals were cut to pieces trying to resist the invaders, leaving survivors who had a greater desire to achieve social cohesion.

Before exile the population of Judah, by then a small nation run from Jerusalem, was swelled by escaping survivors from the destruction of Israel by Assyrians some two centuries before. This forced two strains of religion into close proximity – an older, rustic creed, tolerant of idol-worshipping neighbours and inclined to an organic view of life, opposed by a firebrand fundamentalist elite centered on the Temple in Jerusalem.

In a situation analogous, possibly, with Northern Ireland today, there was no possibility of two rival traditions coalescing into a mutually acceptable dogma.

There were a lot of holy texts that did not enjoy universal acceptance (for instance, the Book of Enoch), and others, without which the mainstream passages, such as those in Exodus, did not make sense (for instance, the lost Book of Jasher). Furthermore, there were subtle and not so subtle variations in mainstream texts. Even in Babylon, the survivors of rival factions would have resorted to more than a little dentistry before agreeing on the final shape of the Hebrew Bible.

The Jews lived within the Persian sphere of influence until Alexander for nearly three centuries. As Persia collapsed suddenly and unexpectedly, it did not develop a lengthy tradition of gloom and doom.

But like all holy libraries composed over such a long period, the Hebrew Bible contains many contradictory messages and moods. Its books composed before the exile are riddled with gloomy sentiment. The glorious era when God nurtured Jewish kings lay in distant antiquity. The last chapters penned before the Babylonian invasion reflected contemporary reality – Judah was a tiny sliver of territory sandwiched between regional superpowers. Its survival depended on constant vigilance, immaculate sense of political balance and a steady supply of miracles.

Most of the essential moral lessons in the pre-exile books of the Bible are to do with fearing God (expect a swift retribution for transgressing against Him) and strictly obeying His instructions. Everything else appears to be flexible, if not unpredictable: some sinners appear to be forgiven whereas others receive savage punishment. Overall, human beings are portrayed as very imperfect creatures. God is forever being driven to ill temper by design flaws manifest in people, especially of the Chosen variety.

That view of man is what Puritans took away as the main message and accepted verbatim. They assiduously ignored parts of the Old Testament that advise man to enjoy life while he can.

Today Jewish religion celebrates humanity, hope and redemption, starting with very specific prescriptions for enjoying life (such as relaxing, feasting and having sex on the Sabbath). There is an optimism that starts with survival of each day, culminating with the expectation of the Messiah.

It is a legacy of Jews from ancient Iran, who rode waves of sustained progress much as their American descendants ride such waves today. Persian Jews were a well-organized, successful community with friends in high places.

It is not surprising if theirs was a totally different outlook on life to that of their ancestors, the ragged ayatollahs of Judean hills. Alas, holy texts of many generations are not easily edited out of the Bible, and addition of new chapters to the sacred library is no simple matter either. Nevertheless, the Jews of Achaemenid era managed to dilute the "crime and punishment" sentiment with something more descriptive of their rags-to-riches reality.

That part of the message the Puritans did not absorb. They found it easy not to see the Persian affirmation of human dignity, ordained by God not only loving but caring of His creation. For too many centuries Christians equated suffering and abasement with goodness. Under the Roman aegis, pleasure was firmly identified with Satan, not God, and Reformation utterly failed to address that legacy.

Nevertheless, the Puritans crystallized many essential elements of Zoroastrianism implicit in the Bible's message – productivity and order being the basis of Puritan redemption.

Both ancient Iranians and modern Americans thus share the same vision – Satan constantly snaps at the heels of the righteous, but his defeat is inevitable with their aid.

Dragon's teeth – the evolution of democracy and capitalism from Indo-European social structures

Despite being unknown by name, the Iranian heritage that Alexander has sought to erase has eclipsed the legacy of Greece. Despite the better propaganda enjoyed by Greek culture, the broad thrust of the Zoroastrian moral system is more representative of modern Western civilization. Despite the repression of Zoroastrian ideas, the persecution of its followers and the attempts to keep Zarathushtra out of history books, it proved impossible to keep his ethos out of institutions on which the modern society rests.

Contrary to what we are all taught, Greece is not the cradle of Western democracy. That political order was indeed common in ancient Greece for some five centuries, but it was by no means universal. Likewise, it was not unique in the ancient world – Carthage and Rome were also republics, although no one accuses either of being the cradles of modern values.

Both Rome and Greece eventually discarded all pretences at democracy. Their Germanic successors were traditional tribal autocracies – the ruler was chosen with consent of his subjects. Once he was crowned, anyone could beg the king to listen to reason, but his will was to be obeyed whether he took heed or not. The alternative was to provoke an armed challenge to his rule, a contest that few participants expected to survive.

Instead, modern democracy originates in Scandinavia, and its practitioners spread that custom by sheer accident. They busily pillaged lands still reeling from the collapse of Roman order. The Vikings were entirely ignorant and contemptuous of any values the Graeco-Roman civilization once espoused.

Viking democracy was based on the same premise as any system of tribal enfranchisement: one hairy warrior with a big axe is, statistically, as good as another in a fight. Settling disputes by a contest at arms is likely to lead to unacceptable losses of valuable manpower, and small communities of hairy warriors soon find themselves under pressure to develop a more "civilized" mechanism of conflict resolution.

Thus arose the Scandinavian institutions of popular assembly, trial by jury and universal rule of law, violations of which unite all hairy warriors against the rogue perpetrator.

By way of perspective, it may be noted that all ancient democracies evolved in the setting of a warrior class, either a separate caste or one that encompassed all males of fighting age. For instance, Carthage was a republic ruled by a senate of one elected hundred men from wealthy families – precisely as in Rome.

On the surface that may seem surprising, since Phoenicians who founded Carthage knew nothing but a long tradition of despotic rule. But the backbone of the new colony was a warrior class – as in Scandinavia, a Carthaginian male was, a priori, an armed sailor, who doubled as infantry in combat. Carthaginian traders were entirely on their own, sailing as far as the West Coast of Africa in small numbers. Only their swords protected them from robbery and enslavement.

In this sense, Rome was a land-based replica of Carthage. Every citizen of the Roman Republic was, first and foremost, a member of the citizen army not unlike that of modern Israel or Switzerland, where promotion in the army tends to mirror one's social ascent. Each Roman male was expected to fight without material reward and be available for instant mobilization over and above any other commitment. A discharge from that liability was a humiliating rite of infirmity or old age, death in battle being a preferred alternative to being an ex-soldier.

Greek city states began as tyrannies, being ruled by a single thug. Democracy was forced on these states by no lofty ideal – rather, a gradual emergence of citizen warriors as a class made it impossible to govern without at least a token attempt at consensus. Greek democracy was practised by many (not all) mainland cities in

Greece, but seldom by Greek colonists, even those in opulent circumstances (such as Syracuse). Pluralism waned in most city states even before they were formally annexed by Rome (187-123 BC).

Stripped of lofty ideals attributed to it by modern Europeans, Greek democracy was not at all what we may imagine today. It was profoundly cynical and corrupt, practising and praising the arts of demagogy (manipulation of the crowd through deceptive oratory) and open thuggery (such as intimidation of rivals or coordination of noise to drown out their speeches). Greek orators prided themselves from being able to argue any point of view with apparently equal logic and conviction, the concept of right and wrong being laughably irrelevant. It is not at all surprising that by Alexander's time much of Greece was lapdog to a Macedonian king, even if democratic process was nominally still in place as a mechanism of local government.

Watching the antics of olympic contenders from the city of Thebes, Alexander asked, with contempt, where thes stalwarts were when his father's soldiers scaled the walls of their city.

The traditional Roman senate was a far more productive assembly where personal interests had to be declared, and all those present were visibly mindful of their responsibility as helmsmen of the state. To place personal interests over those of Rome was – at least in theory – a grave and reprehensible departure from expected conduct.

Under the Germanic model that came to dominate Europe after the eclipse of Roman power, the monarch was elected or otherwise chosen for life. It was not necessarily a hereditary post because a king had to be approved by the people. Even when Scandinavia was long Christianized and fully integrated with the feudal order in Europe, her kings had to take the trouble to tour each district of their kingdom to formally seek the consent of the people to be governed.

The Germanic king had to serve as a judge during the popular assemblies as well as preside over sacrifices. There was an undercurrent of divine ordainment, with kings often claiming a descent from a god.

But in the main, a Germanic king was a military leader. "For life" consequently meant a few years, given that wars were fought as close combat engagements, into which the king led his forces from the front. Given the frequency of war, an unsuitable king was no great problem – anyone hard-done by him could look forward to drowning that grievance at the king's wake, an event that was never more than a few years away.

Germanic and Roman traditions became entangled, the kings of post-Roman Europe gaining not only divine sanction of the church, but also the right of hereditary succession without popular endorsement. That pushed the role of consultative assemblies right off the stage in most countries of mediaeval Europe. Exceptionally, states such as the Venetian Republic or the Hanseatic League did not have a crowned monarch. But these examples should not be mistaken for any form of pluralism, with leaders appointed for life and through mechanisms that had little to do with the asking the man in the street.

There was no set Germanic institution such as an electoral college or a senate for choosing the leader. With a harsh climate, smaller populations and a greater need for social cohesion, the Scandinavians evolved beyond this relatively haphazard system. They came up with a formal people's assembly whose powers were not supplanted by any executive officer, be it a captain of a ship, a commander of a trade colony or a king of a newly united tribal federation.

Living in stark environments like Iceland, the Scandinavians were under heavy pressure to optimize social cohesion. The result is more or less the modern concept of how a free individual relates to society at large, with a fine balance of restrictions, rights and obligations. Most crucially, the Nordic tradition emphasizes equality before the law (which is even a Scandinavian word in English).

Obedience to personal authority of a leader was an entirely voluntary act, in that anyone who did not like the present management had the option of sailing elsewhere. In the Viking Age there was a large surfeit of spare land, especially in Northern Europe. Much of Europe suffered relative depopulation, with vast tracts of land, if not precisely vacant, easy pickings for any military unit.

Such ability to export trouble enhanced the taste for social harmony at home. Scandinavia was truly destined to be the origin of a modern relationship between the individual and the state. For all the blood spilled during the Viking Age, very little of it was shed in Scandinavia herself.

When Scandinavians took to global "back-packing", the model of consensual government had to be extended into their military hierarchy, where it proved an evident success. In effect, the Vikings were a highly motivated citizen navy of an expansionist society, even without a central government to coordinate such massive expansion. Scandinavian marines enjoyed exceptional success against larger forces, until technology made Viking tactics obsolete.

Coalescence of free-standing Scandinavian communities into conventional kingdoms was still centuries away. Meanwhile, egalitarianism ruled – a man with wealth or power still depended on his community for physical survival. A ship's owner planned and commanded raiding voyages, but there was no question of having a hierarchy that would have officers use separate latrines from enlisted men. With only a few dozen sailors in each ship, an individual hated by the leader still had to be treated with respect because others might come to his defence.

Scandinavians thus developed most of the legal institutions familiar to us today – popular assembly shaping a legal system from which no man can be exempt, and a trial by jury of his peers. In Iceland (whose sagas preserved very detailed information about the legal process during Viking Age) cases appeared to be tried before a panel of judges appointed by the assembly: there was usually an accuser and an accused. Most cases were in the format of "civil litigation" – when serious criminal acts were committed, justice was expected to be dispensed by the relatives of the victim without recourse to the assembly. The bench, however, could decree an individual as an outlaw, which stripped him of all privileges of a citizen and made him as vulnerable as any wild animal.

Violence and other interference with the smooth conduct of the assembly invited collective fury – which those who disrupted that important institution deserved. Such disruptions were, not surprisingly, rare.

The modern adversarial format of common law trials comes directly from Scandinavian courts. The Roman version of adversarial process was quite different, and it subsequently evolved from an instrument of civil law into a system of ecclesiastical adjudication during Middle Ages, that operated in a similar manner to the religious police of modern Saudi Arabia. By the time of Reformation all Roman conventions suffered a heavy toll because of their association with the Roman church.

That created a niche for the revival of a lay advocate. He was originally a well-spoken friend or a relative, as amply documented in the Icelandic Sagas. Only later had he become a professional lawyer.

The Vikings did not know or care about the sophistry or the shouting contests of Greek democracy, where the object was to carry a motion and damn the consequences. The Scandinavian version was a very different form of pluralism, one that recognized the fragility of communal survival. A spin of the globe shows which form of democracy proved more enduring.

The Scandinavians did not know or care about the Zoroastrian precedent either. Their system of checks and balances had evolved from practical considerations, rather than as a logical outcome of an ethical system. Scandinavians did not know morality, in the modern sense of the word – they had Germanic law, in which transgressions are treated as a cause to seek revenge or compensation by the wronged party. Germanic tribesmen saw immoral acts as rife with practical and local consequences, rather than offences against a cosmic balance.

Early Scandinavia was a diametric opposite of the post-Roman world it invaded. There the Vikings found states with absolute powers, where those entrusted with the business of the state were unaccountable and open to corruption. That must have amused the Vikings no end, for they exploited the weakness created by such misgovernment all over Europe. Their axe-blows proved the inferiority of its old order, toppling uneasy equilibria perched on the rubble of Roman institutions. The consensual Viking way was, ironically, spread through Europe by force, as its proponents repeatedly won against more sophisticated, more numerous and better-equipped enemies.

The Viking tactics were three-fold – surprise, speed and terror. They did not just overcome resistance and take what they came for, making a point of rape, torture and seemingly senseless destruction.

Yet such actions were no mere acts of unrestrained bestiality. For instance, Vikings did not practise these tactics in Russia, where such methods quickly proved counterproductive. The

Vikings came into Russia from the Baltic Sea, sailing the enormous, slow-flowing Russian rivers to the Black Sea and the beckoning lights of Constantinople. These were long voyages through foreign land, and they the natives were too much of a threat to provoke their hostility. There was fighting with the natives along the eastern shore of the Baltic, but it soon came to an end – obviously, the locals were up to the challenge. After that the Vikings changed direction, concentrating on raids in Western Europe without trying again in the east.

It is evident that unrelated traders and pirates were able to adhere to a common policy of not angering the natives. Relations were surprisingly cordial – so much so that the natives called upon the Rus clan (originally from Sweden) to rule over them – a probable gambit to end costly bloodshed between adjacent tribes by inviting a party of outsiders, too strong and too wealthy to be intimidated or bribed into taking sides.

In most places where they settled Vikings left an extensive cultural trace – another Indo-European blitzkrieg, now using fast ships rather than chariots or armoured horses. Russia has taken much of its pre-Christian culture from the Viking sailor-soldier-merchants.

That legacy included democracy – Novgorod, the second-largest city in Russia, was a genuinely pluralistic republic. Not surprisingly, it was also a powerful entity militarily, relying on free men fighting as volunteers, self-financed and self-disciplined – a social stratum that could not be trod on by the state.

An entirely new chapter in the history of Western Europe began when a large contingent of Vikings, more akin to a credible expeditionary force than a bandit party, sailed up the Seine into the heart of terrified France. They made the return journey with a royal writ ceding the maritime province we now know as Normandy. Its new owners, known to history as Normans (North Men), were still an elite warrior class six generations later, when they arrived to take England. Their French language, which they spoke but crudely, confuses many as to who they really were.

Normans did very much more than conquer England. They came to dominate France and established another outpost kingdom in Southern Italy. By the time of Crusades Normans were the warrior elite of Western Europe – now on horseback, but still comfortable at sea.

Norman nobles spearheaded the blitzkrieg into the heart of Arab world, taking Jerusalem in 1099. Had the rest of the spear been of the same quality as the spearhead, that weapon would have been driven through the Middle East, and Islam would have perished as a global power in the twelfth century. But Europe of that time had nothing like the industry or the population to inflict a serious injury on its Muslim rival, and the Crusades amounted to little more than wild adventure with lasting cultural, but not territorial, benefits.

Viking colonies such as York (set up by Danish Vikings) once dotted England, and their eventual acquiescence to local Saxons did not extinguish their free spirit. When the Normans arrived to claim England, the greatest opposition to their rule came from the long-established yeoman class. The Norman knights found it a rude surprise, for it did not exist in other feudal countries.

A Norman king was nothing more than the strongest amongst his fellow cutthroats. Accordingly, William the Conqueror had no illusions about trying to present himself as a divine figure to his fellow Normans. But his successors began to forget themselves, and this caused a series of confrontations between the crown and its nobles. The culmination of these conflicts resulted in the king being forced to affirm the Scandinavian principle of equality under the law in writing, as Magna Carta of 1215.

With an aristocracy that was never a mere fodder to its kings and an insolent public insistent on having rights in addition to obligations, England was a logical place for the first European revolution. She deposed and executed her king – not for being a king, but for being a bad one – and proceeded to crown his son in the hope that he would be a better servant of public interests.

There were parliaments in many mediaeval nations, consultative bodies modelled on the Senate of Imperial Rome. Most of these were little more than rubber stamps of the monarch, the true ruler. They are not antecedents of European democracy either – a parliament with real teeth is a British institution, which spread to other European countries only in the last two centuries.

Most modern parliaments have been set up using the constitutional monarchy of Britain as a model – not surprising, given that the British system operated with obvious and profound success since the English Civil War.

Historically, the nobility were the first to force the crown into sharing power. Then came the commoners – in the end, English democracy evolved to prevent a dangerous accumulation of resentment among those who could topple existing order.

Europe that emerged from Black Plague and the wars of Reformation was a place where most grown men were proficient in the use of common weapons, and a significant percentage had experienced wartime service. Gone were the days when a charge by a few armoured riders could disperse a crowd of pitchfork-wielding peasants. Sophisticated warfare was now the province of the skilled commoner, voluntary participation and self-imposed discipline. Those who provided this service also had to be allowed to voice dissatisfaction.

That exacerbated the traditional danger of the warrior class – now the entire populace had the ability to organize itself into an army. A crowd of angry English yeomen who shout their anger in a market square can, in short order, march as a coherent military force: armed, officered and coordinated at a moment's notice – as they did in the English Civil War.

Finally governments had to govern entirely with the consent of middle class, even if by nineteenth century most of its males were neither in possession of military-grade weapons nor military training. The American Revolution marked the end of an era in which citizens routinely possessed sufficient training and arms to retool themselves into an army that can win a war against a professional force.

As one can deduce from the German militarization of 1930's, the Indo-European middle class can return to its traditional predestination with lightning speed. Even though ordinary citizens cannot own tanks, bombers or heavy guns, Hitler gave this phenomenon considerable thought. One of his first actions in office was introduction of stringent gun control, which effectively disarmed the civilian population.

To this day, armies check the excesses of dictators and even elected parties, who rule only so long as the army is prepared to tolerate them. Russia is a fascinating study of an interaction between the Indo-European autocrat and his military.

The Czarist army has caused the crisis that led to the 1917 revolution, by widespread desertion and mutiny on the Eastern Front. The old regime collapsed when the same began to occur in the ranks of the police and troops stationed on Russian soil. A remnant of the army, spearheaded by its officer corps, fought the mutineers, united by the Bolsheviks, in a devastating civil war. Skilfully fanned by foreign powers to maximize the damage to Russia, that conflict (1918-1922) indeed saved Europe from Soviet expansionism (attempts at which began even before the Civil War ended).

Stalin developed an elaborate system of control over his military machine, for he could see the problem right away. The Civil War ended with the Red Army taking Crimea, the last of its opponents being hastily evacuated by an Anglo-French flotilla. But as soon as hangovers lifted, Stalin found himself staring down a brand-new military aristocracy composed of Red Army commanders, each with sufficient personal following to overturn the new regime.

In response, the Father of All Nations instituted a system of rapid turnover. The top echelons in every Soviet institution of importance were mowed down on a constant basis, with promotion of new leaders at speed that prevented them from developing interpersonal networks capable of sustaining a coup.

Stalin also split his armed forces into the army proper and *NKVD* (troops of the interior), which divided the ownership of military resources. *NKVD* possessed artillery, tanks and even planes. During World War II *NKVD* troops were tasked to follow army units to prevent retreat, let alone desertion, by liberal use of machine-guns. Political officers (commissars) were tasked to shadow commanding officers, watching for early signs of insubordination and other forms of incorrect behaviour. As a finishing touch, Stalin encouraged both institutions to be at each other's throats.

Stalin's system held up at the point of maximum danger. In 1945 the Red Army was the world's largest military force. Unlike its Czarist predecessor, it was highly trained and disciplined. Armed to the teeth, it was also a recent veteran and victor of a savage conflict.

Its highly popular supreme commander, Georgiy

Zhukov, would have made an even more brutal despot that Stalin. However, Zhukov resisted whatever temptation he had for mounting a putsch and confined himself to a prolific set of memoirs. The reason, no doubt, was something other than adoration of his boss.

But subsequent Soviet leaders didn't have the stomach for Stalin's methods: *NKVD* was disarmed, leaving the Red Army as the sole armed force with real firepower. It is no surprise, therefore, that the army ended up being the undertaker of USSR – as soon as soldiers refused to put down an anticommunist uprising, the regime was gone within days. Under Stalin's system, the tanks on the streets of Moscow would have belonged to *NKVD*, and 1991 would not have seen the end of the Soviet regime – not, at least, with only three casualties.

Stalin, unlike his successors, understood that democracy does not arise when a nation with teeth and claws evolves into a more effete society. He knew that pluralism is not a result of bourgeois weakness. Quite the opposite, it is a way to prevent the warrior caste from turning its weapons against an established order. In the absence of democracy that task can only be achieved through systematic practice of terror.

Democracy was always a highly successful meme; freedom, representative government and individual dignity are highly addictive.

Whenever local circumstances impinged on these rights, Indo-Europeans were not slow to emigrate in search of virgin territory on which egalitarian order may be re-established. That was a major motive amongst the founders of United States, and it is possible that Vikings were no different. We know little about pre-Christian Scandinavia, but its early chroniclers (admittedly, hostile observers) described it as a place of constant and graphic violence, whose inhabitants would be easily tempted to seek a more orderly environment.

A tradition of egalitarianism also pays major dividends when it comes to effective military action. Democracies are not free of military adventures and resultant costly mistakes, but when push comes to shove, in a pluralistic society a commander is reluctant to totally disregard opposing opinions (which any commander is entitled to do). This tends to prevent predictable mistakes.

Stalin learned, within weeks of the German invasion, that he will lose the war by being on the wrong side of the fine line between leadership and interference. Hitler never understood that vital difference – had he done so, Nazi Germany would have been with us to this day.

The meme of democracy thus rode the Indo-European meme to great success – genetically, all existing democracies are inspired or forced by Indo-European societies.

Modern pluralistic society is a coalescence of Scandinavian democracy with Zarathushtra's model of universal morality. Zoroastrianism alone could not shape a complex imperial society into an entity that valued humanism and pluralism. The best it could produce was a cohesive and powerful society, which made the most of its resources – a considerable achievement by ancient standards, but not a suitable substrate, as we saw in Sassanian times, for further social progress.

Humanistic society grew between the scars of late mediaeval Europe, a field ploughed by and fertilized by centuries of war. It was a society that grew hungry for a more effective system of production and government. Its potential cried for something greater than an armed truce between the ruler and the middle class.

The critical mass was achieved during the Puritan Revolution, when armed Scandinavian democracy met the ideology of universal morality and productivity. The result was a lasting and an unprecedented success in turning an Indo-European juggernaut away from destruction, towards peaceful and law-abiding productivity.

Zoroastrian seeds finally found their way into the foundation of a powerful and sustainable society.

Modern capitalism evolved as an institution that strives, mostly with historical success, to channel competition between movers and shakers away from bloodshed.

Societies without a distinct warrior class have no need such channelling – in the setting of ingrained despotism, the ownership of production and resources is not contested by packs of hungry veterans. In ancient Egypt, for instance, there was no warrior class: social ascent was possible only through acquisition of wealth. Suitably qualified noblemen were expected to become army officers, not the other way around. The Pharaoh was commander-in-chief, and he was often entirely unprepared and unsuited to this role.

Capitalism, as it evolved over the past four centuries, could pass for something that was designed by Zarathushtra in person. Modern free enterprise creates a tolerant society that tries to minimize overheads imposed by ideological excesses (which are still amply possible in a democracy). Systemic crime is inimical to efficient business, and environmental sustainability is all to those who depend on the environment for a living. Modern capitalism depends on a comfortable and safe middle class to spend its wages without fear of tomorrow, and that can only occur in stable, predictable environments.

A welfare system, accepted by most capitalist societies today, relieves social pressures that endanger acquisition of wealth. Furthermore, citizens of modern democracies based on free enterprise are encouraged to be proud owners of their national institutions, to contribute not only their taxes, but personal effort and vigilance to maintain public order. These principles, of course, are under increasing pressure from various directions – but they are the principles still.

The Zoroastrian spirit of this design is not coincidental. The single most important agency in the evolution of feudal Europe into a conglomerate of capitalist democracies remains the English Puritan movement, and we already saw where that movement sought its ideological inspiration.

Recent decades saw the rise of numerous supra-national structures such as NATO and the European Union – relatively successful attempts to avoid conflict between fellow Indo-Europeans. Through bitter experience the latter had learned that wars between them are appallingly destructive. It is no longer acceptable or viable to start such conflicts for profit.

There are many reasons why the European Union should be economically and otherwise unviable. Yet, it has been a great success to-date. Those who abstained from it the longest were nations with no recent memory of a destructive invasion. Those who rushed into this structure headlong tended to have bitter experience of wars with neighbours, and they proved willing to sacrifice economic and chauvinistic considerations in the hope of deterring future wars between Europeans.

It is possible for the Arab world to live in an armed stand-off with Israel, a conflict that occasionally erupts with limited loss of life on either side. This permanent state of low-level war has major economic and political benefits for "front-line" Arab societies, and they will lose handsomely if the conflict is ever resolved.

No such low-level war is possible between Russia and Germany – any future exchange of fire between these nations is likely to set off another global cataclysm. The last such misunderstanding began in 1914 and only ended, by rights, in 1991, with the official collapse of USSR and evacuation of Soviet troops from Germany. Any noteworthy battle between Germans and Russians had cost more lives in one day than all of the Arab-Israeli conflicts put together.

It is no coincidence that nations without a warrior caste are reluctant converts to the new world order, which expects them to hold elections and build economies. These societies are structured differently – kleptocrats grow fat on corrupt exploitation of natural resources, keeping the populace in check through quasi-judicial terror. Without a warrior class there is no obvious alternative to the existing kleptoelite – all challengers come from within, unless a major effort is exerted from outside to upset this structure, as happened in Iraq on numerous occasions.

The old Indo-European ways enjoyed a fatal culmination during the twentieth century. That, along with failure of Communism and the collapse in the authority of the church, proved pivotal in the conversion of many countries towards democracy and capitalism. Simply, the alternatives are now known to be too frightening.

To highlight this point, it is worth examining one alternative path, one that presents an ongoing temptation, even for tried and true democracies.

Conceived as a revival of Rome, the Italian fascist republic was structured into a logical outcome of Indo-European society – a merciless state with iron-fisted control over its population. The purpose of that state is to be at war – anywhere, by any means and with any consequences, so long as the military-industrial-cultural complex is maintained.

Although fascism is traditionally ascribed to Hitler (who called himself something quite different, a nationalist socialist), it is entirely the brainchild of Benito Mussolini, who assumed power and "restored order" nearly a decade before Hitler.

The German doctrine of racial superiority had nothing to do with Mussolini's fascism (indeed, Goebbles ruefully referred to Italians as politically sound but racially unsound). Ironically, German Nazism was a radical departure from the way Aryans did business since the heady days of Kurgan Culture – they much preferred to convert the citizens of any race or creed to their culture, rather than exterminate them on the basis of a racial difference. The Italian fascism was far closer to the spirit of Proto-Indo-European expansion.

Mussolini's fascism succeeded in becoming an Indo-European state taken to its logical extreme: a war-mongering government, hand in hand with a military-industrial complex, the national culture saturated by a state-sponsored ideology, praising brute warriors above any other category of citizen.

Fascism should never be dismissed as a threat. It remains an eternal temptation for any struggling society. Experience, ancient and modern, suggests that a creation of a militaristic state on the substrate of a potentially powerful society is a highly effective means of social mobilization. It is interesting to theorize how long Mussolini would have lasted without Germany's world war. Quite conceivably, his creation could live on for a number of generations. Resurrection of Roman imperial power was an exceptionally seductive vision, not to mention effective political model, at least in the short term. Under Mussolini Italy experienced a major economic and cultural revival after centuries of neglect and plunder. It is a sobering fact that Churchill once called Mussolini the genius of Rome.

The only superpower left standing today was also founded by admirers of ancient Rome, who copied Roman institutions deliberately and openly. They were true to the spirit of their times, when ancient Rome and Greece were held as ideal societies that created ideal citizens. The founding fathers of America enlisted many Graeco-Roman ideals to the task of building the new republic.

But their view of Rome was fatally blinkered by idealization of Graeco-Roman culture. It is not a coincidence that two centuries later, the federal government of that superb nation is beginning to resemble a hostile fascist overlord of small democratic states, just as Roman Caesars once ruled over the hapless "friends of Rome". Nor is it a coincidence that at federal level the ruling body of United States of America increasingly resembles a parody on the eponymous Roman Senate, also dominated by a corrupt and clannish oligarchy.

For the time being, Americans still elect their

Caesars, but it is not something they should take for granted – that would repeat a grave error of their Roman predecessors.

Rome herself was originally an oligarchical republic. Whilst the population nominally chose the senators, they all came from the same class – the patricii. The situation is similar in modern USA – all American presidents to-date were white, male and mostly born into wealth. The overwhelming majority had military experience, followed by a career in big business. Clinton was the first notable exception to that pattern in his century, born in a trailer park and rising through sheer talent and determination. He never served in uniform, and he never even inhaled. Which is no shame as, presumably, Monica never inhaled either.

When Caesar Julius used his popularity with the legions to install himself as dictator, Romans acquiesced with remarkable speed. There were attempts to restore the republic, but they lacked popular backing – not surprising, as the republic was seen as a corrupt dictatorship of the wealthy, which was delivering poor results for the man in the street.

Only a short time later Augustus, the nephew of Julius, defeated the last of the rival contenders for his uncle's position. A return to republicanism was already neither realistic nor much desired by citizens, not slow to appreciate the efficiency of an autocrat, who was at that point competent, decisive, relatively humane and honest.

By Nero's time the once-great senate was reduced to a consultative assembly, with the monarch making all decisions and bearing all responsibility for the outcome. There is no physical reason why the same sequence cannot play out in United States of America, profoundly distracted from its raisons d'etre by a war against fleas and rodents in the dark corners of our planet.

Finally, there are many Indo-European societies that have known neither genuine democracy nor sustainable capitalism – for instance, Iran and Russia. These societies are viable and even powerful, if not inclined or even able to apply their power to the benefit of their people.

That reminds us that the Indo-European recipe for success does not rely on respect for human rights, free enterprise or even due process. These are recent and optional additions to the basic design of Indo-European culture.

Nevertheless. In the last one hundred years humanistic values, first promulgated by a Bronze-Age prophet, had purchased a reliable hold on in the world's wealthiest and powerful countries.

It is cause for hope.

Epilogue: a personal note.

Is the obscurity of Zoroastrianism an accident?

I say it is more. That religion requires a genuine commitment to personal morality – a quality that humanity attempted to supplant with two millennia of a State-sponsored God, who works hand in hand with earthly tyranny.

Modern Zoroastrians show little inclination to share their ethical system. Given the condition of host societies, it is not difficult to see why they should be so inclined.

What can an adherent of Zarathushtra's principles say to those who destroy family life and make whores out of their scholars, judges and soldiers?

What can someone who takes pride in the painstaking labour of generations say to the modern-day servants of Satan, who immolate products of human endeavour at orgies of political correctness?

What would Zarathushtra say about the modern version of a nomadic raid – a state that taxes productive inheritors of Bronze Age farmers at the behest of those who hijack material wealth by manipulation of public emotion?

Above all, what is the point of explaining Zarathushtra's creed to a society that has industrialized the process of lying?

But as we speak, the world convulses.

It is an undeniable that most traditional religions are losing followers – with the possible exception of Islam, whose adherents still enjoy reproductive advantage over their religious rivals. Whatever the rights and wrongs of these religions, a golden age of civilizations founded on devotion to them is clearly past.

Christian society saw its apogee some century and half ago, and modern fundamentalists of Islam are busy inviting an apocalyptic disaster upon their world in its entirety. Their challenge to the Western world can only result in appalling consequences along the lines of Carthage.

Traditional Judaism, Hinduism and Buddhism can hardly claim credit for the quality or the manner of life of their followers. That credit largely goes to the emulation of Anglo-American ways by the respective societies. It may be said that neither of these religions can convincingly claim a positive influence on the nature of societies that profess them. Their moral practicality is therefore suspect.

Humanity even tried worshipping a moral vacuum, but it is hard to suggest that it was anything other than resounding failure, which saw nations of the former Soviet Union descend into bestiality for an entire century. An opposite culture of the West, with its goal of endless consumption and conveniently relativistic morality, is increasingly recognized as a failure.

Social orders that supplant individual responsibility are rapidly nearing the end of their sustainable life. These failures are crying out for a return to a code of behaviour with the highest immediate overheads – but greatest sustainability in the long run. It is a simple and harsh morality that boils down to a demand that each sentient being cleans up his own mess.

As governments world over grasp at more power yet weaken with every turn, the scene is set for a return to a simpler way. It is most ironic that such a way was there all along, quietly biding its time since the dawn of Bronze Age.

All alternatives have been exhausted to a moral code that confronts each individual with a choice: practise decency and responsibility – or live the results of being without them.

A universal acknowledgement of this simple truth – along with recognition that good cannot result from condoning evil – may or may not be what Zarathushtra envisaged as the apocalyptic victory of good over evil.

But three and a half thousand years later, I cannot think of a better way to defeat Satan and cast him back into void.

IBE

1999 – 2007

A modern symbol of Zoroastrianism

Selected Bibliography

1. Aldred C: Akhenaten: King of Egypt 1991 0-500-27621-8

2. Allan T, Phillips C, Kerrigan M: Wise Lord of the Sky: Persian Myth Myth and Mankind, 2000 Duncan Baird Publishers 2000 ISBN-10: 0705436330

3. Avari B: India: The Ancient Past: A History of the Indian Sub-Continent from c. 7000 BC to AD 1200 2007 ISBN-10: 0415356156

4. Barber EW: The Mummies of Urumchi 1999 ISBN-10: 0393045218

5. Boyce M: History of Zoroastrianism: Volume 1, The Early Period Handbook of Oriental Studies/Handbuch Der Orientalistik 1996 ISBN-10: 9004104747

6. Boyce M: Textual Sources for the Study of Zoroastrianism Textual Sources for the Study of Religion 1990 ISBN-10: 0226069303

7. Boyce M: Zoroastrians: Their Religious Beliefs and Practices Library of Religious Beliefs & Practices 2001 ISBN-10: 0415239036

8. Bradford E: Hannibal Wordsworth Military Library 2000 ISBN-10: 1840222263

9. Brent P: The Mongol Empire 1976 ISBN-10: 029777137X

10. Brown RA: The origins of modern Europe, 1972 ISBN-10: 0094580006

11. Byock JL: Viking Age Iceland Penguin History 2001 ISBN-10: 0140291156

12. Casson L: Travel in the Ancient World 1994 ISBN-10: 0801848083

13. Cavalli-Sforza LL: Genes, Peoples, and Languages 2001 ISBN-10: 0520228731

14. Cavalli-Sforza LL: The Great Human Diasporas: The History of Diversity and Evolution Helix Books ISBN-10: 0201442310

15. Chunakova OM: Zoroastrian Texts Russian Academy of Sciences 1997 (Russian)

16. Cook JM: Persian Empire 1994 ISBN-10: 0226627772

17. Dawson MM: The Ethical Religion of Zoroaster 1931 ISBN-10: 0766191362

18. del Castillo BD, Cohen JM: The Conquest of New Spain Penguin Classics 1963 ISBN-10: 0140441239

19. Douglas D, Clanchy MT: The Normans 1976 ASIN: B000UOHFL8

20. Eisenman R: The Dead Sea Scrolls and the First Christians: Essays and Translations 2004 ISBN-10: 0785818855

21. Fraser A: Cromwell Our Chief of Men 1989 0-7493-0107-4

22. Geoffroy-Schneiter B: Gandhara. The Memory of Afghanistan - 2001 ASIN: B000NUL1QY

23. Ghirshman R: Iran Pelican 1978 ISBN-10: 0140202390

24. Glubb JB: A Short History of the Arab Peoples 2007 ISBN-10: 0812813510

25. Glubb JB: Soldiers of Fortune: The Story of the

Mamelukes 1973 ISBN-10: 0880292474

26. Grant M: History of Ancient Israel 1996 ISBN-10: 0297817701

27. Grousset R: The Empire of the Steppes: A History of Central Asia 1988 ISBN-10: 076070127X

28. Hamilton JR, De Selincourt A: The Campaigns of Alexander Penguin Classics Arrian, J. R. 1976 ISBN-10: 0140442537

29. Hanson VD: Why the West Has Won 2002 ISBN-10: 0571216404

30. Herodotus: The Histories Penguin Classics Aubery de Selincourt Translator ISBN-10: 0140449086

31. Hinnells J: Persian Mythology 1975 0-600-03090-3

32. Hodgkin T (Ed): Barbarian Invasions of the Roman Empire 8 Volumes 2000 ASIN: B000UDGZV0

33. Hyland A: Training the Roman Cavalry: From Arrian's Ars Tactica Military Series 1993 ISBN-10: 0862999847

34. Irving C Crossroads of civilization: 3000 years of Persian history 1978 ISBN-10: 0064932389

35. Jones G: A History of the Vikings 2001 ISBN-10: 0192801341

36. Lancel S, Nevill A: Carthage: A History 1994 ISBN-10: 1557864683

37. Lieu S: From Constantine to Julian 1996 ISBN-10: 0415093368

38. Mallory JP: In Search of the Indo-Europeans: Language, Archaeology, and Myth 1991 ISBN-10:

0500276161

39. Man J: Attila the Hun 2006 ISBN-10: 0553816586

40. Matheson SA: Persia an Archaeological Guide 1976 ISBN-10: 0571048889

41. Mazar A: ARCHAELOGY OF THE LAND OF THE BIBLE Anchor Bible Reference Library 1990 ISBN-10: 038523970X

42. Moscati S: The Phoenicians 2001 ISBN-10: 1850435332

43. Olmstead AT: History of the Persian Empire Phoenix Books 1959

44. Olson S: Mapping Human History: Genes, Race, and Our Common Origins 2003 ISBN-10: 0618352104

45. Pearlman M: The Zealots of Masada: Story of a Dig 2004 ISBN-10: 9652800740

46. Plutarch: Lives Volume 1 Modern Library Classics 2001 ISBN-10: 0375756760

47. Rawlinson HG: Bactria, The History Of A Forgotten Empire 1892 ISBN-10: 8120616154

48. Rawlinson HG: PARTHIA ISBN-10: 160206136X 1893

49. Renfrew C: Archaeology and Language: The Puzzle of Indo-European Origins 1990 ISBN-10: 0521386756

50. Sayce AH: The Hittites: The Story of a Forgotten Empire 2005 ISBN-10: 1402174489

51. Stevens R: The Land of the Great Sophy 1979 ISBN-10: 0413457907

52. Stoyanov Y: The Other God: Dualist Religions from

Antiquity to the Cathar Heresy Yale Nota Bene 2000 ISBN-10: 0300082533

53. Syme R: The Roman Revolution 2002 ISBN-10: 0192803204

54. Tafazzoli A: Sassanian Society 2000 Bibliotheca Persica Press 0-933273-48-7

55. Tanner S: Afghanistan: A Military History from Alexander the Great to the Fall of the Taliban 2003 ISBN-10: 0306812339

56. Wallis WD: Religion in Primitive Society 1939 ASIN: B000P723DU

57. Wood F The Silk Road: Two Thousand Years in the Heart of Asia 2004 ISBN-10: 0520243404

58. Xenophon: The Persian Expedition Penguin Classics 1950 ISBN-10: 0140440070

59. Zaehner RC: The Dawn and Twilight of Zoroastrianism Phoenix Press 2003 1-84212-165-0